SOUTH AFRICA
in Pictures

Janice Hamilton

Lerner Publications Company

Contents

Lerner Publishing Group realizes that current information and statistics quickly become out of date. To extend the usefulness of the Visual Geography Series, we developed www.vgsbooks.com, a website offering links to up-to-date information, as well as in-depth material, on a wide variety of subjects. All of the websites listed on www.vgsbooks.com have been carefully selected by researchers at Lerner Publishing Group. However, Lerner Publishing Group is not responsible for the accuracy or suitability of the material on any website other than <www.lernerbooks.com>. It is recommended that students using the Internet be supervised by a parent or teacher. Links on www.vgsbooks.com will be regularly reviewed and updated as needed.

Website address: www.lernerbooks.com

Lerner Publications Company
A division of Lerner Publishing Group
241 First Avenue North
Minneapolis, MN 55401 U.S.A.

web enhanced @ www.vgsbooks.com

Library of Congress Cataloging-in-Publication Data

Hamilton, Janice.
      South Africa in pictures / by Janice Hamilton.—Rev. & expanded.
         p.   cm. — (Visual geography series)
      Summary: Text and illustrations present detailed information on the geography, history and
government, economy, people, cultural life, and society of traditional and modern South Africa.
      Includes bibliographical references and index.
      ISBN: 0-8225-0938-5 (lib. bdg. , alk. paper)
      1. South Africa—Juvenile literature. 2. South Africa—Pictorial works—Juvenile literature. [1. South
Africa.] I. Title. II. Visual geography series (Minneapolis, Minn.)
DT1719.H36 2004
968'.0022'2—dc21   2002156560

Manufactured in the United States of America
1 2 3 4 5 6 - JR - 09 08 07 06 05 04

INTRODUCTION

South Africa is a land of great beauty, from the skyline of Cape Town to the peaks and ravines of the Great Escarpment. It has a variety of landscapes, from the savannas of Kruger National Park to the flowers that bloom in arid Namaqualand. This vast country at the southern end of the African continent is rich in minerals and agricultural resources. It has the best-developed economy in sub-Saharan Africa. Politically, it is a well-functioning democracy. And for the first time, the black majority, whites, Indians, and people of mixed ancestry are trying to build their country's future together.

Little more than a decade ago, South Africa was an international outcast. Its apartheid system, which classified citizens according to race and kept the different races apart, was condemned by the international community. The nation's white minority ran the government, industry, and the farming sector. Meanwhile, members of other ethnic groups suffered from institutionalized racism and a bleak standard of living.

South Africa's indigenous (native) Khoisan people were hunter–gatherers and herders. By A.D. 200, black farming people had begun to move into the eastern regions from farther north. These people usually spoke one of a group of similar languages that became known as Bantu. Europeans set up their first settlement in 1652 in what later became Cape Town. People of Dutch, French, and German origin later moved into the region and became known as Afrikaners. British colonists arrived in the 1800s and competed with the Afrikaners for land and political influence. Both the Afrikaners and the British pushed the Khoisan and the black Africans off the land. In the 1900s, whites set up a system, known as apartheid, that deprived people of color of their human rights.

Many groups, including the black-led African National Congress (ANC), objected to apartheid. As a result, the country saw years of political protest and violence until President F. W. de Klerk and Nelson Mandela, ANC leader, negotiated a new South Africa. In 1994 all

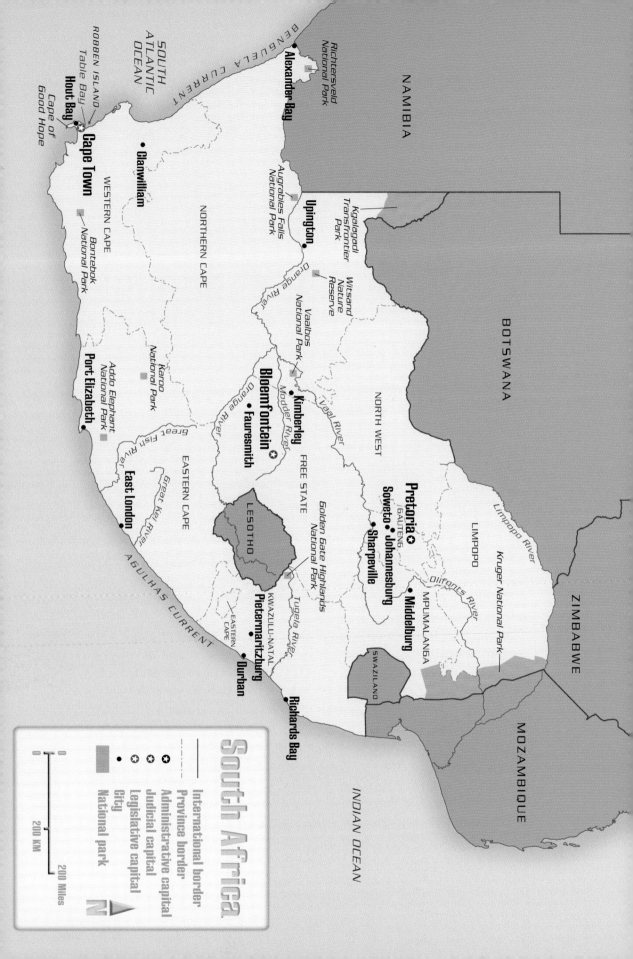

South Africa

International border
Province border
Administrative capital
Judicial capital
Legislative capital
City
National park

0
0
200 KM
200 Miles

N

SOUTH ATLANTIC OCEAN

BENGUELA CURRENT

Richtersveld National Park

NAMIBIA

Alexander Bay

ROBBEN ISLAND
Table Bay
Hout Bay
Cape of Good Hope
Cape Town

WESTERN CAPE

Bontebok National Park

Glanwilliam

NORTHERN CAPE

Augrabies Falls National Park

Upington

Kgalagadi Transfrontier Park

Witsand Nature Reserve

Orange River

Vaalbos National Park

BOTSWANA

NORTH WEST

Vaal River

Limpopo River

LIMPOPO

Kruger National Park

ZIMBABWE

Karoo National Park

Port Elizabeth

Addo Elephant National Park

Great Fish River

Orange River

Bloemfontein

Fauresmith

Kimberley

Modder River

FREE STATE

Golden Gate Highlands National Park

LESOTHO

EASTERN CAPE

Great Kei River

East London

Pretoria
GAUTENG
Soweto
Johannesburg
Sharpeville

Middelburg

MPUMALANGA

Olifants River

Limpopo River

KWAZULU-NATAL

EASTERN CAPE

Pietermaritzburg

Tugela River

SWAZILAND

Durban

Richards Bay

INDIAN OCEAN

MOZAMBIQUE

AGULHAS CURRENT

Nelson Mandela *(center)* **and F. W. de Klerk** *(right)* accept the 1993 joint Nobel Peace Prize for their roles in the peaceful dismantling of apartheid.

South Africans—black, white, and otherwise—had the right to vote for the first time. Mandela was elected president.

Even though the dismantling of apartheid without a full-scale civil war was an extraordinary event, South Africa will need years to recover from the effects of the apartheid policies. Many people suffered physically and emotionally from their experiences. Apartheid also left the country with great economic disparity. Some South Africans have a standard of living equal to that of the world's wealthiest nations. Yet millions more South Africans live in extreme poverty. These people—mostly blacks—lack housing, clean water, electricity, and schools. The country's crime rates are among the highest in the world.

While the nation tries to deal with these social and economic challenges, the human immunodeficiency virus (HIV), the virus that often causes acquired immunodeficiency syndrome (AIDS) poses a very serious problem. Population growth is expected to decline due to the huge numbers of people infected with the disease. Communities and families are losing young leaders. The government has been slow to introduce a program to treat patients in the public health system with anti-AIDS drugs. HIV/AIDS prevention programs may finally be starting to have an effect, however. Meanwhile, the government faces criticism for not dealing effectively with the crisis.

THE LAND

With an area of 472,856 square miles (1,224,692 square kilometers), South Africa is about twice the size of Texas. Its 3,045-mile (4,900-km) northern border meets Namibia, Botswana, and Zimbabwe in the north and Mozambique and Swaziland in the east. South Africa entirely surrounds the independent Kingdom of Lesotho. South Africa's 1,790-mile (2,880-km) coastline faces the Indian Ocean to the south and east and the Atlantic Ocean to the west.

South Africa is divided into five geographic regions. The largest region, the Plateau, sits about 8,000 feet (2,440 meters) above sea level in the east. It gradually descends to the north and west. The Highveld, the largest of the Plateau's three subregions, includes the gold-bearing rocky ridge known as the Witwatersrand. The Middleveld in the west is an arid (dry) rolling plain between the Kalahari and Namib Deserts, where depressions (low areas) collect rainwater. The Middleveld is used primarily as rangeland for livestock. The third subregion, the Bushveld, also known as the Transvaal Basin, forms the country's

northeastern corner. It consists primarily of rolling grassland and thorny bushes. At its northern edge, the Bushveld becomes a series of plateaus and low mountains that drop into the Limpopo River Valley.

Forming a semicircle from the east to the southwest, the plateau soars into the Great Escarpment. This series of mountain ranges that run parallel to the coast includes the Drakensberg Range, where the country's highest point, Champagne Castle, at 11,070 feet (3,375 m), is located. The narrow Coastal Strip lies between the Great Escarpment and the Indian Ocean. The strip runs from the border of Mozambique to the Cape Mountains Region and varies in width from about 35 miles (60 km) to more than 125 miles (200 km).

The Cape Mountains Region in the south and southwest is a series of mountain ranges of very old, folded rock. Some of these ranges extend in a north-south direction, while others are oriented from east to west. The Great Karoo, an arid plateau, separates the Cape Mountains from the Great Escarpment.

White sand dunes up to 180 feet (60 m) high give **Witsand Nature Reserve** its name. It is part of the otherwise rusty red Kalahari Desert.

South Africa's two other geographic regions are deserts. The Namib Desert faces the Atlantic Ocean and continues across the Namibian border. The vast Kalahari Desert, stretching from north of the Orange River into Namibia and Botswana, features wind-blown ridges of rusty red sand.

◉ Rivers

The 1,240-mile-long (2,000-km-long) Orange River is South Africa's most important waterway and one of the longest in Africa. It originates in mountainous Lesotho, then drops to the veld (grassland), where it flows through wide valleys and narrow gorges. At the spectacular Augrabies Falls, it splits into several channels and descends into a long ravine. Its final rugged tract marks the border with Namibia before it enters the Atlantic near Alexander Bay.

No large towns are located along the Orange River's banks. Sandbars, rapids, and a highly variable flow make it useless as a transportation route. But it is important for irrigation. Grapes, alfalfa, and dates grown along the banks of the lower Orange contrast with the nearby desert. The massive dams, reservoirs, canals, and tunnels of the Orange River Project provide both hydroelectric power and irrigation.

The murky, gray Vaal River rises in the eastern province of Mpumalanga and flows southwestward for about 745 miles (1,200 km) until it joins the Orange. The Orange's other main tributary, the Caledon, merges with the Orange near the Gariep Reservoir.

The region north of the Witwatersrand ridge is drained by the 1,120-mile (1,800-km) Limpopo River, which forms South Africa's borders with Botswana and Zimbabwe. The waterway loops northeastward from its source in the Witwatersrand before crossing into Mozambique on its way to the Indian Ocean. The wild and remote Tugela River begins in the Drakensberg Range and empties into the Indian Ocean north of the city of Durban in KwaZulu-Natal province. A dam near Ladysmith controls its flow. The southern parts of the country, including the Great Karoo and Cape Mountains regions, are drained by a number of short rivers. South Africa has no large natural lakes.

Climate

Because South Africa is in the Southern Hemisphere, winter lasts from June to August. January through March are the summer months. The country has a mainly temperate (mild) and dry climate. Ocean currents and elevation are the primary influences on weather patterns. On the Atlantic side, an atmospheric phenomenon known as the Benguela Current sweeps cold winds northward, keeping the west coast of South Africa cool and dry. The Indian Ocean's warm Agulhas Current flows south, bringing warmer temperatures and more rain to eastern South Africa. Durban, on the east coast, has an average annual temperature of 70°F (21°C), while the area at a similar latitude on the west coast has an annual average of 57°F (14°C).

Elevation influences temperatures, so that the city of Pretoria, on the Highveld, while inland and farther to the north, has similar temperatures to coastal Cape Town. Average July (winter) temperatures are 54°F (12°C) in Cape Town and 52°F (11°C) in Pretoria. Average January (summer) temperatures are 69°F (20°C) in Cape Town and 72°F (22°C) in Pretoria.

Summer temperatures in the north often exceed 90°F (32°C), and parts of the Northern Cape and Mpumalanga provinces have reached record highs of 118°F (48°C). In the mountains, winter daytime highs may reach 50°F (10°C) to 70°F (21°C), but temperatures sometimes fall below freezing overnight. Winters are warmer on the eastern and southeastern coasts. In winter, air from Antarctica often brings rain.

Rainfall varies across the country. The driest regions are in the west, where the Namib Desert gets almost no rain. The Cape Peninsula has a wetter climate, with enough winter rain to make agriculture possible. Subtropical conditions prevail on the east coast, which gets about 40 inches (100 centimeters) of precipitation a year.

At sunset a **thunderstorm** crosses a nature reserve near Pretoria.

South Africa's national flower, **the king protea,** can grow to 1 foot (0.3 meters) in diameter. Visit vgsbooks.com to learn more about South Africa's flora and fauna.

⊙ Flora and Fauna

South Africa has several different biomes, or ecological zones, including the unique Fynbos. This 27,000-square-mile (70,000-square-km) area, which lies in the southwestern part of the country, encompasses the Cape Floral Kingdom, one of the world's six distinct floral kingdoms. Its more than 8,500 species of flowering plants are native only to this area. The low, hardy plants of the Fynbos grow in a variety of habitats, from salty marshes to mountain slopes.

The savanna, or Bushveld, with mixed grasslands and camel thorns, baobabs, and spekboom trees, is home to large mammals such as lions, elephants, and zebras. In the grasslands zone, wild currant trees and thorny acacias are mainly found near rivers or on hillsides, and animals such as black wildebeests and elands thrive.

Several types of vegetation survive in South Africa's semidesert areas. One zone supports hardy shrubs and grasses. In the western part of the country, another zone is known for its wildflowers and succulents (plants with thick, waxy leaves that retain moisture). These regions provide habitat for small animals such as bat-eared foxes and ground squirrels.

South Africa's indigenous forests are home to giant yellowwood and ironwood trees. Some forests are thick with ferns and lichens. Small forested areas are found in the mountains of the eastern escarpment and on the east coast. Many forest animals, including the Cape parrot and the samango monkey, are endangered.

GARDEN TRANSPLANTS

Many flowering plants that grow naturally in South Africa are familiar in gardens around the world. Geraniums, campanulas, lobelias, and plants with bulbs such as freesias and gladioli are among the many species that have been successfully transplanted to other climates since the 1700s. In modern times, scientists and farmers continue to introduce new garden plants from South Africa to countries around the world.

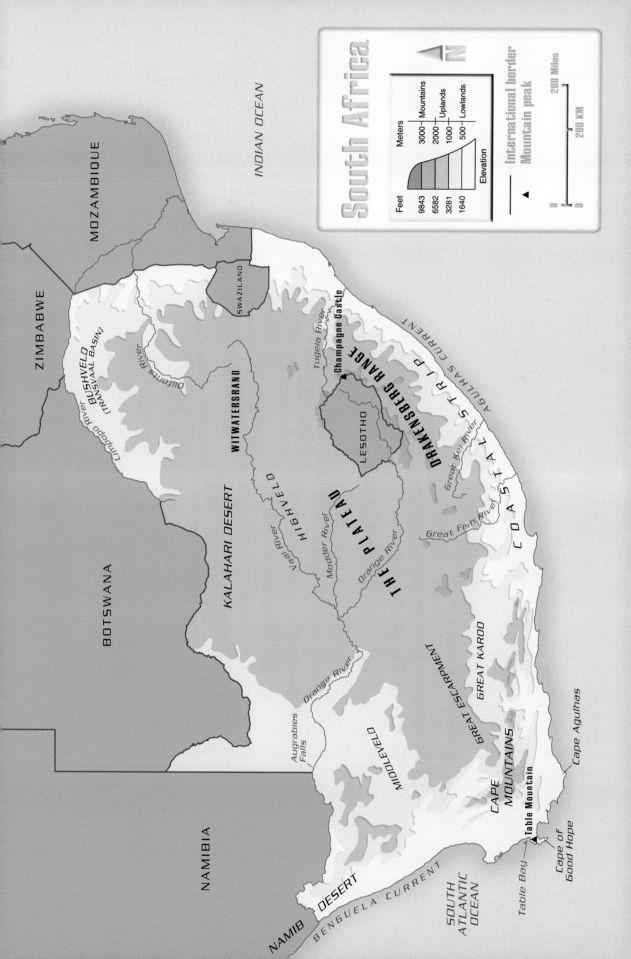

South Africa

ZIMBABWE

MOZAMBIQUE

INDIAN OCEAN

BOTSWANA

NAMIBIA

SWAZILAND

Limpopo River

Olifants River

BUSHVELD
(TRANSVAAL BASIN)

KALAHARI DESERT

WITWATERSRAND

HIGHVELD

LESOTHO

Champagne Castle

Tugela River

DRAKENSBERG RANGE

Great Kei River

Great Fish River

COASTAL STRIP

AGULHAS CURRENT

Vaal River

Modder River

Orange River

THE PLATEAU

MIDDLEVELD

Augrabies
Falls

Orange River

GREAT ESCARPMENT

GREAT KAROO

CAPE
MOUNTAINS

Table Mountain

Cape of
Good Hope

Table Bay

Cape Agulhas

NAMIB DESERT

BENGUELA CURRENT

SOUTH
ATLANTIC
OCEAN

Elevation

Meters		Feet
3000 — Mountains		9843
2000 — Uplands		6582
1000 — Lowlands		3281
500		1640

International border

▲ Mountain peak

200 Miles

200 KM

A **baby elephant** bathes in a water hole in Addo Elephant National Park. At birth an elephant can weigh more than 250 pounds (113 kilograms).

South Africa is probably best known for its "big five" wildlife residents (lions, elephants, rhinoceros, leopards, and buffalo), but the country has an enormous variety of animal and plant life. It is one of the world's most biologically diverse countries, with some 18,000 species of plants, and some 230 species of mammals.

Most of South Africa's land mammals are quite small. Mounds of excavated earth give away the presence of moles in underground tunnels. Most of the country's 75 species of bats eat insects, and several fruit-eating species help pollinate plants. Families of meerkats, relatives of the mongoose, inhabit desert areas, foraging for insects while one member of the pack stands on sentry duty. The national animal, the springbok, is a graceful, horned gazelle. Springboks eat

As the seasons change, **springboks** gather in herds of thousands to move to new feeding areas.

The **secretary bird** can fly, but it rarely does. Instead it may walk up to 20 miles (32 km) each day.

grass and shrubs and survive on arid plains by obtaining water stored in the roots and leaves of succulent plants.

Among reptiles and amphibians are several species of rain frogs, which live underground and do not need water, as well as land tortoises and chameleons. Common birds include hornbills, with their huge beaks, and secretary birds, which prey on snakes, trampling them to death with their long legs. The African hoopoe of the Bushveld—easily recognized by its crested head and black-and-white barred wings—uses its long, curved beak to dig insects out of the ground.

Natural Resources and Environmental Issues

South Africa is rich in mineral resources. It has almost half of the world's gold reserves, which are located primarily in the Witwatersrand. The gold is difficult to mine, however, as it is embedded in rock that lies deep underground.

The country is a leading producer of platinum and gem-quality diamonds. It also has the world's largest known deposits of chromium, manganese, and vanadium (minerals used in the production of steel and other alloys). South Africa is the largest producer of iron ore in Africa. The country also has significant deposits of copper, nickel, lead, titanium, zinc, and other metals and large reserves of uranium, a by-product of gold and copper mining.

Small reserves of oil and gas have recently been discovered off South Africa's coast. Coal mining is relatively easy and inexpensive, and much of the country's large coal supply is burned in generator plants to produce electricity or is converted to synthetic fuel.

Water is scarce in South Africa. Rivers are the main source of water for homes, agriculture, and industry, but many of the country's rivers are in the escarpment, far from heavily populated areas.

Go to vgsbooks.com for links to websites where you can find photos and information on South Africa's cities and landscapes, up-to-date population figures, current weather conditions, and more.

Dams store water and harness it for power and irrigation, as well as help regulate the water's naturally variable flow and transfer it from one area to another.

Fertile land is limited, but agricultural resources are nevertheless an important part of the economy. About 13 percent of the country's surface area can be used for crop production, and many crops require irrigation. About 80 percent of South Africa's farmland consists of natural pasture for feeding sheep and cattle. Only about 1 percent of the country is forested, but wood is grown extensively on plantations. Fish are particularly abundant in the food-rich, cold water of the Atlantic.

Industrial waste and air pollution are South Africa's main environmental challenges. Toxic dust from gold mine waste sites poses a serious health hazard to nearby communities. Mining activities have also left groundwater contaminated with acids and other chemicals. Underground mine shafts have made hillsides unstable.

Most of South Africa's electricity is generated by burning coal. With coal's high sulfur and ash content, the burning process contributes to airborne particles, acid rain, and atmospheric greenhouse gases. Airborne particles of sulfur dioxide, ozone, and industrial smoke cause respiratory problems for urban residents. Wood, coal, paraffin, and dung—burned for heat in winter in badly ventilated homes—also cause respiratory problems.

Pollutants fouling South Africa's long coast include untreated household sewage and industrial waste. Coastal areas are also vulnerable to spills from oil-shipping traffic offshore.

The country has a good record in conservation. It has a well-established national park system and strict laws against poaching (illegal hunting). Still, many species—including 1,700 of the 8,500 flowering plants indigenous to the Fynbos—are rare, vulnerable, or endangered. This is primarily because of habitat loss and competition from invading foreign plant species.

Soil degradation is a serious problem. South Africa's soil is naturally poor, and tons of topsoil disappear annually from wind and water erosion. Many of South Africa's rivers run down steep slopes, increasing runoff and soil erosion. In some rural areas, too many people and livestock are forced to live off too little land, worsening the problem. Meanwhile, the rapid growth of urban areas has reduced wild areas. Farmland has been lost to sprawling suburban developments and squatter communities (illegal settlements).

⊙ Cities

Founded in 1652, Cape Town is the site of the first white settlement in South Africa. The country's Parliament meets in the city. With its dramatic setting between the mountains and the sea, Cape Town is a popular tourist destination and is home to 2.7 million people. The city's main industries include wine making, fishing, chemical manufacturing, and automobile manufacturing. Cape Town is one of the largest fruit-exporting ports in the world.

Johannesburg, with a population of about 2.5 million, is South Africa's second largest city. Founded in 1886 following the discovery of gold, the city is an important commercial and financial center whose mines used to produce 40 percent of the world's annual gold production. But when the price of gold fell in 1989, many of the mines became unprofitable. The majority of Johannesburg's population is black, and most of these people live in townships (communities) outside of the city center. Soweto is the largest of these black townships.

Durban has a total population of almost two million, including a large Indian community. Durban has a large port, connected by road to the industrial Witwatersrand area. Minerals, coal, sugar, and grain are exported, while imports include industrial equipment. Imported oil is refined and sent by pipeline to Johannesburg, and the sugar industry is headquartered there. With warm weather year-round, Durban's beaches and nearby wildlife reserves attract tourists from other parts of the country.

Pretoria, founded by Afrikaners in 1855, is the administrative capital of South Africa. Many of its residents are employed by the government. Pretoria has several universities, colleges, and scientific research centers. Industry is based on steel manufacturing and diamond mining. Located north of Johannesburg, this beautiful city of 1.6 million residents has tree-lined streets and large parks.

The city of **Pretoria** may be viewed beyond the flower gardens of the Union Buildings, which is where South Africa's administrative offices are located.

HISTORY AND GOVERNMENT

Some of the earliest hominids—species that had features of both apes and humans and were the ancestors of modern humans—lived in the region three million years ago. Bones of the hominid species *Australopithecus africanus* have been found at several locations. The discovery of 1.3 million-year-old charred bones in a South African cave suggests a later species, *Homo erectus*, had mastered the use of fire. Between two hundred thousand and forty thousand years ago, the area's *Homo sapiens*, or modern human beings, gradually shifted from using clumsy stone tools to more sophisticated spearpoints, scrapers, and finely crafted tools. These people lived in open camps or under rocky overhangs and hunted medium-sized prey such as antelopes. Eventually, people in the area domesticated livestock and herded their animals over large areas. These people came to be known as the Khoisan.

Farmers who had moved in from farther north had established agriculture in South Africa's eastern regions by the A.D. 200s.

These farmers spoke closely related Bantu languages in which variations in tone of voice can give words different meanings.

By the 1500s, three groups of indigenous people were living in what later became South Africa. The majority of the Bantu speakers had settled in the eastern part of the region. Meanwhile, two distinct groups had descended from the Khoisan. The San were hunter-gatherers and lived predominantly in the west. The Khoikhoi raised livestock mostly in the south and west.

Arrival of the Europeans

Strong currents and the lack of harbors made South Africa difficult to reach via the ocean. As a result, southern Africa was isolated from non-African influences and contacts for many centuries. In the 1400s, European nations searched for ocean routes to Asia to participate in the lucrative spice trade. Portuguese explorers first reached the region. In 1488 Bartolomeu Dias rounded the Cape of Good Hope (an extension of land jutting from the southwest coast of Africa) and anchored briefly off the southern coast of the continent. In 1497 Vasco da Gama followed the coast around the southern tip of the continent to the coast of Eastern Africa, opening a trade route to India. Despite southern Africa's treacherous seas, many Portuguese, English, Dutch, French, and other merchants sailed around the Cape over the next century. Some merchants set up trading companies to finance trade between Europe and India.

During the 1600s, the Dutch East India Company was the most successful European trading company in the area. In 1652 the company sent a small group of employees, led by Jan van Riebeeck, to establish a refreshment station at Table Bay. The station's residents had hoped to acquire meat, fresh fruit, vegetables, and other necessities from the local Khoikhoi. The settlers would then provide these goods to ships passing on the long route between Europe and India. But as more ships began using the route, the Khoikhoi were not able to meet the increasing demand. The Dutch then decided to turn the refreshment station into a colony. The station came to be known as Cape Town, and the settlement surrounding it was named the Cape Colony.

To make room for settlers, the Dutch forced the Khoikhoi out of the area beyond the Cape Colony. The Khoikhoi moved into the interior, where they had to compete with the San for land. Many also died from smallpox, a disease carried by European travelers. Additional European settlers arrived, including French Huguenots

Table Bay, near modern Cape Town was named for the flat-topped mountain *(center)* at its shore.

Jan van Riebeeck (shown in this statue in Cape Town) is credited for founding the city, but the Dutch East India Company had not instructed him to start a permanent colony. His orders were to build a fort and to grow fruits and vegetables for the crews on passing ships.

who were escaping persecution for their Protestant faith. The Dutch brought in slaves—captured Khoikhoi and people imported from Madagascar, Mozambique, Malaysia and other parts of Asia—to do most of the manual labor.

The settlers also moved onto lands occupied by the San. As skilled hunters, the San strongly resisted and fought the Dutch throughout the 1680s. But with superior technology, the Dutch defeated the San, who were forced to move to other regions, including the Kalahari Desert.

The Cape Colony continued to grow over the next century. By 1793 the colony had 13,830 Dutch-speaking residents and 14,747 slaves. Many of the white semi-migrant farmers, or *trekboers,* had difficult lives. Some lived in crude, clay-walled houses, far from Cape Town. They periodically traveled to the city to sell sheep, cattle, and butter to pay for essentials such as guns, tea, sugar, and tobacco. Trekboers were dependent on the labor of slaves.

The British Cape Colony, the Mfecane, and the Great Trek

By the late 1700s, the British navy had become the world's dominant sea power. The British had established colonies in North America, India, and other locations. Seeking a safe route to India for their ships, the British captured the Cape in 1795. With the help of the trekboers, British forces drove the indigenous Xhosa out of the area.

These defeats at the hands of the white settlers were part of a long and difficult period for the area's black African populations. With white settlements expanding into the interior, space and resources had become limited for blacks. When a long and severe drought began around 1800, many Africans starved. Wars broke out as African groups

By 1824, when the first Europeans arrived in Zulu territory, the Zulu leader **Shaka** (standing left) had quadrupled Zulu territory by using strict military discipline and clever battle plans.

fought over food and water. As a result of these conflicts, several large African states developed. These included the Zulu kingdom, led by the warrior Shaka, who ruled in the 1820s. Other states included the Swazi, the Sotho, and the Ndebele.

Famine and war forced survivors to migrate, searching for food, safety, and land. Roaming groups fought established groups. This period was known as the *mfecane,* a Zulu word meaning "time of troubles" or "the crushing." The large-scale devastation from the conflicts among the African states left white settlers with the impression that few people lived in the areas of the eastern interior.

In 1820 five thousand British settlers arrived in the Cape Colony. The British government had sent them to settle the southeastern region of the country near the Great Fish River. These new settlers created a buffer zone between the rest of the Cape Colony and the black African states to the northeast.

Meanwhile, blacks within the Cape Colony either lived as slaves or were forced to work for very low wages. The Cape's whites classified the Khoikhoi and the former Asian slaves as one group, calling them the "Cape coloured people," despite their many ethnic and cultural differences. In 1834 the British government freed all slaves throughout its empire, including the Cape Colony. Many of the trekboers, or Afrikaners as they called themselves, were angered by this action. These people depended on slavery for their livelihood. Conflict between the British and the Afrikaners continued as the two groups competed for land east of the Cape Colony. Many Afrikaners decided to start a new settlement outside of Cape Town that would be free from British rule.

Beginning in the mid-1830s, about six thousand Afrikaners and an equal number of coloured servants left the Cape Colony. They came to be known as the Voortrekkers. Their Great Trek eventually became part of Afrikaner legend. A large number of the Voortrekkers moved north of the Vaal River, settling in the territory of the Ndebele people. Land disputes brought the two groups to war, and by 1837 the Voortrekkers had driven the Ndebele across the Limpopo River.

Other Voortrekkers moved to the territories northeast of the Cape Colony, creating conflict with the area's Zulu population. In 1838 ten thousand Zulus, armed with spears, attacked five hundred Afrikaners led by Andries Pretorius. The Afrikaners, who had chosen an easily defended spot, suffered no deaths, but three thousand Zulus were killed in what became known as the Battle of Blood River.

The Voortrekkers claimed much of the fertile land south of the Tugela River and established the Natal Republic. The British became concerned that this settlement would threaten the trading port they

A monument in Pretoria depicts a circle of Voortrekker wagons.

had established at Port Natal (modern-day Durban). They responded by sending a force that annexed (took control of) Natal. Determined to remain free from British rule, some of the Voortrekkers moved again, joining other Afrikaners on the Highveld. In 1854 the region south of the Vaal River became the Orange Free State, an independent republic. Farther north, the Afrikaners established the South African Republic, also known as the Transvaal.

Meanwhile, in the eastern regions of the Cape Colony, white settlers and Xhosa farmers clashed over land. This led to a series of wars in the 1840s and 1850s in which the better-equipped whites eventually defeated the Xhosa, burning their villages and crops and seizing their livestock.

While the black African population in the Cape Colony declined through war and famine, the white population experienced significant growth. A census taken in 1865 counted 180,000 Europeans (whites), 100,000 Cape coloured people, and 100,000 Kaffirs (the name whites gave to black Africans who worked as manual laborers). Cape Town and Port Elizabeth (located on the southeastern coast of the continent) were the two largest towns. The population also grew in the colony of Natal, where six thousand laborers from India came to work in the newly planted sugarcane fields. Large numbers of British settlers also arrived, and by 1870, the population of Natal included 15,000 British, 3,000 Afrikaners, and about 270,000 black Africans. In Natal black and white communities were mostly separate.

◉ Diamonds, Gold, and the Boer War

In 1867 people in the region discovered diamonds near the confluence (meeting point) of the Vaal and Orange Rivers. Within a few years, fifty thousand people had converged on the site of the world's largest concentration of gem diamonds. The Voortrekkers had previously claimed the area, but in 1871, the British annexed the diamond fields for their own. In 1877 they also annexed the colony of the Transvaal. But in 1881, the people of the Transvaal fought back and defeated the British army in what the Afrikaners, or Boers, called the First War of Independence.

Meanwhile, the British attempted to take over African land for farming and to force the Africans to work as cheap laborers. The British fought wars against the Zulu, the Griqua, the Xhosa, and others during the 1870s and 1880s. By the mid-1880s, the British had subdued most of the black African population, which lost most of its land. Many black Africans were forced to work as laborers in diamond mines or on white-owned farms.

The Kimberley Mine near Kimberley was first mined for diamonds in 1868. It is known as the Big Hole in modern times for good reason. Workers had removed 22.5 million tons (20.4 million metric tons) of earth from the Big Hole by 1914. Surface mining extended downward about 2,625 feet (800 m), and an underground mine shaft reached a depth of 3,600 feet (1,100 m).

White domination of the region increased in 1886, when prospectors discovered gold on the Witwatersrand, an area controlled by the Boers. Thousands of immigrants from around the world came to work in the mines. A new city, Johannesburg, was established near the mines, and it grew quickly. Coal mining and other service industries developed in the region. Railways were also built, linking Johannesburg to Cape Town and to Durban in the 1890s.

De Beers Consolidated Mines, which British immigrant Cecil Rhodes controlled, acquired a monopoly (exclusive control) of the diamond industry. Through investment in the gold mines, Rhodes also became an important figure in the gold industry. Both industries were structured along racial lines. Only whites held skilled and supervisory jobs, while blacks did the dangerous manual labor. Furthermore, whites lived in communities with their families, while blacks had to live in closed, all-

Cecil Rhodes

male camps, leaving their families behind in their home villages. Whites also created laws to standardize black wages. To keep blacks from moving from place to place and selling their services to the highest bidder, the government required all blacks to carry passes, or permits, to move from one place to another.

As the 1800s came to a close, the British wanted more access to the gold reserves of the Witwatersrand. British businessmen had purchased all of the mines, but the mines themselves were located in Boer territory. The British mine owners hired English-speaking whites to do most skilled labor jobs. But these Uitlanders, as the Boers called them, were denied voting rights in the Boer territories. Boer leaders feared that giving the growing English-speaking population the vote would lead to British domination of the Boer states. Throughout the 1890s, tension grew between the two groups as the British vied for control of the region while the Boers sought to maintain their independence. In 1899 British colonial leaders began massing troops in the Cape Colony for a possible invasion of Boer territory. In response, the Boer states of Transvaal and the Orange Free State formed an alliance and declared war on the British.

For more than two years, the British and the Afrikaners fought, with heavy losses on both sides. Some black Africans also served in the war, with most of them working as laborers for the British army. Although the British had greater access to supplies and soldiers, the Boers countered with hit-and-run guerrilla-style warfare. The British responded by burning Afrikaner crops and farms and by forcing civilians into concentration camps. By the time the British had defeated the Afrikaners, some twenty-eight thousand Afrikaner civilians had died in the disease-ridden camps.

Leaders on both sides signed a peace treaty in 1902, in which the Afrikaner nations agreed to British rule. Many black Africans were disappointed with the treaty. They had hoped the treaty would give them the right to vote and the right to demand better working conditions in

A unit of black South African and British soldiers in the Boer War (1899-1902) lines up for a group photograph.

the Afrikaner republics. But this was not the case. In 1906 Natal's blacks, who outnumbered the whites by a ratio of 10 to 1, rebelled. The Natal militia (citizen army) crushed the uprising, killing three thousand blacks, but whites remained afraid of further violent outbreaks.

The Union of South Africa and the African National Congress

Concerns about black-led violence, combined with a realization that Afrikaners would not abandon their desire for independence, led the British to seek a compromise. In 1910 the British government granted all of the colonies—the Cape Colony, Natal, the Transvaal, and the Orange Free State—self-government within the British Empire, forming the Union of South Africa. The new country was home to 4 million Africans, 500,000 coloureds, 150,000 Indians, and 1.3 million whites. English and Dutch were both official languages. The new government formed an elected British-style parliament, but only white men could vote in the Transvaal and the Orange Free State. In Natal and the Cape Colony, few black Africans or coloureds met the criteria for voters. Seeking to achieve rights for blacks through legal means, a group of educated, middle-class black Africans founded the African National Congress (ANC) in 1912.

But two years later, world events forced many South Africans to set aside domestic issues during World War I (1914–1918). South African troops fought in Europe and East Africa alongside Britain and other countries to defeat Germany and its allies. South African troops also invaded and conquered its northern neighbor, the German colony of South-West Africa (modern-day Namibia).

INDIAN CONNECTION: MOHANDAS GANDHI

Mohandas Gandhi, who later led India toward independence from Great Britain, lived in Natal from 1893 to 1914. When he arrived, he was a young Indian lawyer with no interest in politics. But the humiliating treatment he received in South Africa made him aware of racial issues. Gandhi helped South African Indians organize to fight discrimination and led people in strikes and protests. Although these efforts did little to improve the situation of South Africa's Indian community, they did change Gandhi himself. His concept of nonviolent protest later provided an inspiring example to Mandela and other South Africans of a means to overthrow a ruling power through a peaceful mass movement.

A postcard of four British colonies, including South Africa *(lower left)*, honors their participation in World War I.

Following the war, South Africa and other British colonies pressed the British government for independence. As a result, the British government passed a law in 1931 giving South Africa and several other countries, including Canada and Australia, full control over their own domestic and foreign affairs. At the same time, the British Commonwealth of Nations, an organization that maintains ties of friendship and cooperation between Britain and its former colonies, was created.

These ties again caused South Africa to side with the Allies (Great Britain, the United States, the Soviet Union, and others) during World War II (1939–1945). South African forces served in East Africa, in North Africa, and in Italy. South Africa's ports, mines, manufacturing industries, and farms helped to defeat Germany, Italy, and their allies.

The Apartheid Era

During the war, many black Africans moved from rural areas to urban areas to take jobs in the booming wartime industrial sector. For the first time, in 1946, blacks outnumbered whites in South Africa's urban areas. Yet the government did not want large numbers of Africans in urban areas because they feared they could be a threat to whites. Leading up to 1948, South Africa's white leaders passed a series of laws that gradually restricted the rights and freedoms of the black African people. The government tightened pass laws to try to restrict African travel and to control employment. The laws stated that only blacks who could prove they had jobs could be allowed to stay in the towns. Otherwise, the government required that blacks remain in the countryside. The laws also segregated South Africa's cities, with whites and other races living in different areas.

A strong stance for segregation helped bring the Afrikaner-dominated National Party to power in the national election of 1948. The new government expanded the segregation laws, putting into effect the policy of apartheid, an Afrikaans word that means "apartness" or "separateness." The man largely responsible for these laws was Hendrick Frensch Verwoerd. He served initially as minister of native affairs and later as prime minister. Verwoerd promoted apartheid as "separate development," in which each race would have its own homeland. Whites would run South Africa, but black Africans would rule their own reserves.

The government passed the Population Registration Act, which officially classified everyone as either white, coloured, Indian, or African (black). Marriage and sexual relations between the races were illegal. The act reorganized the reserves into ten homelands, each run by an African hereditary chief who was supported by the white government. The pass laws were again tightened, and Africans working in South Africa were treated as foreign migrant workers. They were not allowed in areas reserved for whites unless they were employed there. Any African who did not have the proper documents could be arrested.

After studying sociology and psychology in Germany during the rise of its Nationalist (Nazi) Party, **Hendrick Verwoerd** became the editor of *The Transvaaler*, a nationalist newspaper in the Afrikaans language. Soon after that, he entered South African politics as a member of the National Party. He became prime minister in 1958.

"Reserved for the use of Europeans only" reads this beach sign from the apartheid era.

Beaches, hotels, town halls, buses, washrooms, schools, universities, and sports arenas were all segregated. Africans lived in sprawling townships on the edges of the cities, traveling to work every day.

Under apartheid, South Africa became a country of increasing extremes. Whites had excellent health services, long life expectancy, and low infant-mortality rates. Africans suffered from diseases common to developing countries, such as tuberculosis, gastroenteritis, and typhoid fever. The homelands experienced outbreaks of bubonic plague and cholera. White children had good schools, teachers, and equipment. Schools for coloured, Indian, and African children lacked basic resources.

Laws kept opponents of apartheid from joining together to stage mass public demonstrations against the system. People who protested against apartheid could be legally held in jail without trial. Critics of the government could be "banned," meaning they could not leave their homes, join certain organizations, or talk to other banned individuals.

Anti-apartheid Efforts

The country's white-owned industries benefited from apartheid, as blacks provided cheap labor. But some white citizens and organizations spoke against the system. All of South Africa's Christian churches, except the Dutch Reformed Church, criticized the system. Other nations denounced apartheid, and beginning in 1952, the United Nations passed annual resolutions condemning it.

In 1955 several groups, including the ANC and Indian and coloured organizations, adopted a Freedom Charter that included calls for racial

Oliver Tambo was a highly respected African leader in the 1970s and 1980s. He traveled the world to educate audiences about the injustice of apartheid.

equality, freedom of speech, and freedom of religion in South Africa. This charter became the basic policy of the ANC. Meanwhile, ANC members elected three educated black leaders—Nelson Mandela, Oliver Tambo, and Walter Sisulu—to lead the organization.

At the same time, a new black organization, the Pan-Africanist Congress (PAC), organized peaceful protests against apartheid. But in 1960 at Sharpeville, near Johannesburg, police opened fire on a PAC demonstration, killing at least 67 people and wounding 186. Following the Sharpeville incident, the government quashed further protest by jailing thousands, by banning the PAC and the ANC, and by proclaiming a state of emergency.

In 1961, facing increasing condemnation by fellow members of the British Commonwealth, South Africa withdrew from that group and became a republic. The same year, a militant branch of the ANC, Umkhonto we Sizwe (Spear of the Nation), began staging terrorist attacks against government and industrial targets. These attacks included setting off bombs in police stations and power plants. In 1963 police arrested seventeen Umkhonto leaders. The next year, Mandela, Sisulu, and six others were tried for treason, sentenced to life, and sent to Robben Island prison. Tambo escaped to lead the ANC from exile in Zambia.

Although they performed hard labor in the lime quarries of Robben Island, Nelson Mandela and his fellow prisoners had a lot of time to think and talk during their imprisonment. The inmates discussed the ideas of intellectual leaders such as Karl Marx and Mohandas Gandhi and the literary efforts of William Shakespeare and traditional African stories. Mandela learned the Afrikaans language from his guards so he could better understand and talk to Afrikaners.

Although the government had halted violent protest temporarily, members of the African community continued to work against apartheid. African writers criticized apartheid in books that were published overseas (such books were illegal to publish in South Africa), and a black theater movement developed in Johannesburg to produce anti-apartheid dramas.

Steps toward Equality

The system itself began to show signs of strain. The white government had underestimated the growth of the black population and the unstoppable flow of migrants to the cities. Furthermore, an unskilled black migrant workforce no longer served South Africa's economic needs.

In response, the government reversed an earlier policy that had made it illegal for blacks to do skilled jobs and increased spending on black education with the aim of creating a more skilled workforce. At the same time, African workers began a series of strikes to demand better working conditions and wages. Some business leaders realized that allowing blacks to form legal trade unions would simplify labor negotiations. The resulting unions formed a core of anti-apartheid resistance.

The anti-apartheid campaign extended beyond South Africa's borders, as many governments chose not to do business in South Africa. Some black South Africans left the country to train as guerrilla fighters in Tanzania and Angola. They returned to stage terrorist attacks on government targets.

Anti-apartheid protesters march in front of the South African Embassy in Washington, D.C., on the twenty-fifth anniversary of the 1960 Sharpeville shootings.

Anti-apartheid protesters burn tires in a township near Cape Town.

Meanwhile, the South African government wanted to stop supporting the homelands. To achieve this goal, it made four of the homelands independent. But rather than benefiting blacks, homeland independence caused more problems. The territories were broken into so many small pieces that they would not have been economically viable. Foreign governments refused to recognize them as independent states. In KwaZulu homeland, Chief Mangosuthu Buthelezi led the Inkatha Freedom Party (IFP), which opposed independence by violent means if necessary.

The 1980s saw frequent violence in the townships, as anti-apartheid protests swelled. With political leaders in jail or organizing sabotage operations from underground, church leaders took a major role in organizing peaceful protest. In 1984 Anglican Church leader Desmond Tutu won a Nobel Peace Prize for his leadership in trying to bring a peaceful end to apartheid.

Some progress was made in 1984 when President Pieter Willem Botha reformed the constitution, creating a legislature that was divided into white, coloured, and Indian houses. But blacks, who represented 75 percent of the population, remained excluded. Yet the new laws repealed the ban on interracial marriages and allowed blacks into white universities. Identity cards, which all South Africans had to carry, replaced the black-only passes.

But even these signs of progress couldn't disguise the fact that apartheid was crippling South Africa's economy. A severe drought and fluctuations in the price of gold, in addition to strikes and political uncertainty, harmed business and investment. The high costs of administering different services for each ethnic group and of controlling the unrest took their toll. International economic sanctions and a severe drop in foreign investment were also stalling economic growth.

The End of Apartheid

Mandela, whose reputation as a leader had grown while he was imprisoned, received frequent visits from foreign officials who supported the anti-apartheid struggle. The ANC began holding secret discussions with business leaders in 1985, and with the government in 1987, to discuss the dismantling of apartheid. Mandela participated in these talks, but the government still sought a means for whites to keep some measure of power. In 1989 President Botha suffered a stroke and resigned. His replacement, F. W. de Klerk, began the process of dismantling apartheid.

In 1990 de Klerk announced that public facilities would be desegregated. That same year, he lifted the ban on the ANC and other anti-apartheid groups. A few days later, Nelson Mandela was released from prison. Representatives of nineteen different organizations began meeting in 1991 to discuss a new constitution. In 1992 de Klerk called for a referendum (vote) in which whites were asked to reject or approve the new politically integrated South Africa. They overwhelmingly approved change. The relatively peaceful and fair election of 1994 gave the ANC 62 percent of the vote, and the National Party took 20 percent. On May 10, 1994, Nelson Mandela, age 76, was sworn in as president. He set up a multiracial cabinet that included members of several parties. International sanctions were lifted, and South Africa was welcomed back into the international community, rejoining the United Nations and the British Commonwealth.

To heal the wounds of apartheid, the government set up the Truth and Reconciliation Commission to investigate human rights abuses that had occurred between 1960 and 1994. Chaired by Archbishop Desmond Tutu, the commission began hearings in 1996. Some twenty-one thousand victims, activists, informers, and police gave testimony. The final report, which appeared in 1998, said that the government had violated human rights and that former president P. W. Botha and IFP leader Mangosuthu Buthelezi were responsible for a variety of violent acts. The report emphasized that the fight against apartheid had been a legitimate liberation movement. Yet it held the ANC's militant wing and the PAC accountable for human rights violations and the deaths of civilians.

Archbishop Desmond Tutu

After Mandela

After serving one five-year term, Mandela chose not to run again in 1999 as ANC leader. Thabo Mbeki replaced him as ANC leader and became president when the party retained a large majority in the National Assembly.

But South Africa's leaders face many difficulties. Huge social and economic challenges remain to be solved. Nine million South Africans, most of them black, still earn less than a dollar a day. On average, black workers earn one-tenth the salary of whites, and 50 percent of blacks do not have steady employment. South Africa is also experiencing a severe health crisis, particularly with HIV/AIDS. And many South Africans regard crime as one of the nation's most pressing challenges.

Despite the massive changes that took place in their society, South Africans have not entirely reversed their racial attitudes. Distrust between blacks and whites continues, and the different groups still live socially separate and economically unequal lives. Yet with a troubled past clearly behind it, South Africa is bracing itself for the challenges of the future.

Government

The Republic of South Africa adopted a new constitution in 1996. The constitution establishes a democratic state, founded on the principles of equality before the law and of the advancement of human rights and freedoms. It provides for a number of fundamental human rights to protect individuals from discrimination on the basis of gender, race, ethnic origin, religion, disability, and sexual orientation.

South Africa has a bicameral (two-house) Parliament, consisting of an elected National Assembly and a National Council of Provinces. The head of state is the president, who is elected by the National Assembly from among its members. Each of South Africa's nine provinces selects ten delegates to the National Council of Provinces.

Each province has an elected legislature headed by a premier. The provinces have responsibility for some areas of government and share power with the central government in areas of national interest.

South Africa's judicial branch oversees the court system. The constitutional court consists of eleven members and is headed by a chief justice. The president appoints the members, and each serves one seven-year term. The court's duty is to make sure that all the branches of government adhere to the constitution when making decisions. The court may override decisions made by the National Assembly. A supreme court and a number of provincial courts decide criminal and civil cases.

THE PEOPLE

The estimated population of South Africa is 43.6 million. The nations population density of 92 individuals per square mile (238 per sq. km) is misleading, since populated regions are unevenly distributed. Most of the semiarid interior and western areas have very small populations. Farm homes in areas such as the Karoo can be miles apart. On the other hand, KwaZulu-Natal and Gauteng provinces are densely populated.

Some 23.4 million South Africans—about 54 percent of the population—make their homes in urban areas. Most live in major cities such as Johannesburg, Cape Town, and Durban. Others live in smaller cities and towns, which act as regional administrative, farming, or industrial centers.

South Africa's cities have experienced high growth rates in recent decades. Africans who had lived as tenants on white-owned commercial farms were forced to leave between the 1960s and the early 1990s. Also, the migrant labor system, once part of apartheid,

continues to draw men from rural areas to the cities. Some 15 percent of black South African men and 5 percent of black South African women spend at least one month per year away from home for work.

⊙ Ethnic Groups

The South African population is 77 percent black. South Africans of European descent make up 11 percent of the population. Coloureds represent 9 percent, and Asians account for 3 percent.

Among African ethnic groups are the Nguni-speaking people, who account for about two-thirds of the African population. Nguni speakers include the Zulu, the Xhosa, and the Ndebele, who form the majority in eastern and coastal regions. Sotho-Tswana people live primarily in Highveld areas. The Tsonga are concentrated in Limpopo and Mpumalanga provinces, while the Venda come from Limpopo province.

Historically, African ethnic groups mixed with each other through marriage and conquest. When the government tried to impose tribal identities on the different groups as part of apartheid, the Africans themselves did not go along with these ethnic classifications.

The majority of South Africa's whites are descended from Dutch, French, German, and British settlers. To a large extent, the English-speaking and Afrikaans-speaking communities remain socially separate. South Africans include people of Portuguese and Italian origin and a small Jewish community.

The apartheid government made a separate category of South Africans of mixed race, calling them coloureds. Living mostly in the Western Cape province, they are the descendants of unions between slaves, whites, Africans, Khoisan, or a combination of these people. Over the centuries, they became socially isolated from both the European and the African communities. Most speak Afrikaans, and most are Christian. Other Cape residents include the Cape Malays, who are descended from slaves from the Dutch East Indies (Indonesia) and Madagascar. Many have kept both their religion and Asian musical traditions. The term Khoisan is used to describe descendants of two groups—the San, the indigenous hunting-gathering people, and the Khoikhoi, the original herding people of the region.

Most Asian South Africans have ties to India. Many maintain strong cultural roots.

Indian-run open-air stalls, such as this one in Durban, are a common sight in urban South Africa. They cater to a large Indian population.

They came as merchants or to work on the sugarcane plantations in the 1800s. Their descendants live primarily in towns and cities of KwaZulu-Natal province.

In the early 2000s, several million new immigrants, mostly from neighboring countries such as Mozambique and Zimbabwe, have arrived in South Africa. Some are refugees fleeing civil unrest. Others have come to South Africa in search of work.

Language

South Africa has eleven official languages: Zulu, Xhosa, Afrikaans, Pedi, English, Tswana, Sotho, Tsonga, Swazi, Venda, and Ndebele. Citizens can use their language when dealing with a national government employee, and a member of Parliament may address Parliament in any official South African language.

The African languages, most of which are members of the Bantu family of languages, coincide with ethnic groupings. Zulu is the primary tongue of 23 percent of the population, followed by Xhosa (18 percent), Afrikaans (14 percent), Pedi (9 percent), and English (9 percent).

Most government communication appears in English. But the government promotes the use of African languages by giving ten of the most widely spoken languages official recognition. The constitution states that persons have the right to be taught in the language of their choice whenever reasonably possible. Many people speak several African languages as well as Afrikaans and/or English.

AFRIKAANS

About seven million people in South Africa and Namibia speak Afrikaans. Afrikaans, meaning "African" in Dutch, includes words from many origins, although 95 percent of the language stems from Dutch. After three centuries in Africa, the language has incorporated influences from Malayan slaves, from other European languages, and from indigenous African languages.

Afrikaners are not the only South Africans who speak the language. Half of all Afrikaans speakers are black, although most speak a dialect of Afrikaans. To distance Afrikaans from its racist past, some people are investigating its multilingual roots and highlighting the diversity of speakers and dialects.

Learn a few basic words in some of the country's eleven official languages by going to vgsbooks.com. You can also find out more about the various customs of people in South Africa— including the Zulu, Xhosa, and others.

On this fence in Soweto, **an AIDS awareness message** *(left)* joins signs about the value of education and the leadership of Mohandas Gandhi.

Population Growth and Health Trends

South Africa is a youthful country. An estimated 34 percent of its residents are younger than fifteen years old. Only 5 percent of the population are over sixty-five. Many parents who work in the cities send their preschool-aged children to stay with relatives in rural areas.

Most countries in Africa have steady increases in population. But because of high death rates, South Africa's population is expected to decline to 35.1 million by 2025 and to 32.5 million by 2050. Should these predictions become reality, South Africa will experience a total population decrease of 25 percent from 2001 to 2050. Yet modern medical facilities have meant the infant mortality rate of 57 deaths for every 1,000 live births is much lower than that of other sub-Saharan countries.

The key factor in South Africa's population decline is HIV and AIDS. Some 4.2 million South Africans are living with the virus. HIV/AIDS has had a major impact on life expectancy. Projected life expectancy in 2015 for South Africans with HIV/AIDS is 37 years, compared with 70 years for those who do not have the disease. Average life expectancy at birth is 52 years for men and 54 for women.

AIDS has become the leading cause of death in South Africa. In the early 2000s, it accounted for 1 in 4 deaths and for 40 percent of deaths that occurred in people between the ages of 15 and 49. A report by the South Africa Medical Research Council predicted that AIDS will kill between 5 and 7 million South Africans by 2010 unless measures are taken to control the epidemic, which primarily affects the impoverished black community. About 2 percent of the white population have HIV/AIDS.

The disease has devastated communities, killing young people who should be active in the workforce and orphaning at least three hundred thousand children. The number of children to lose their parents to the disease is expected to reach two million by 2010. Young mothers pass on the disease to their babies at birth.

AIDS first appeared in South Africa among white homosexual men in the early 1980s and did not affect the segregated African population. In the early 1990s, black immigrants arrived from nearby countries where AIDS was a problem. From that point on, the disease spread quickly. Many men, especially those who work in the city while their wives stay in the country, have multiple sexual partners. Most men consider condoms (which can prevent transmission of the disease) unmanly and refuse to wear them. But AIDS awareness programs are gathering strength in South Africa. Some large companies and unions have organized their own prevention and treatment programs for their employees.

Some 56 percent of married women of childbearing age practice family planning, mainly through birth control pills. In 1996 the government adopted a law that gave women of any age or marital status access to abortion services upon request during the first twelve weeks of pregnancy.

South African women have the primary responsibility for raising children. Many women effectively head their families because their husbands have left them or live and work elsewhere. Female-headed households often earn half the average income of male-headed households. Day-care programs are not available in most black communities, but female family members often share child-care responsibilities.

South Africa has a relatively modern health-care system and large city hospitals. But a disparity exists between health care for whites and nonwhites. Many white people have private medical insurance and receive good medical care. Most blacks depend on public healthcare services provided by the government. Due to high demand and lack of

In 1967 at **Groote Schuur Hospital in Cape Town,** South African surgeon Dr. Christiaan Barnard performed the world's first human heart transplant.

TRADITIONAL MEDICINE

Many South Africans consult a traditional healer before they go to a doctor who practices Western medicine. Traditional healers use medicines derived from plants and animal parts and may use trances or throw bones on the ground to diagnose the patient. Healers are often influential members of their communities. Doctors sometimes try to work with them, to teach them how HIV is spread or to persuade them not to give a powerful herb that will make a patient vomit a Western medicine.

adequate funding, these facilities do not provide the same quality of health care as private medical providers. Many rural black people do not have any access to health care because facilities are too far away. Meanwhile, the massive HIV/AIDS epidemic is stretching the country's health resources, and diseases such as tuberculosis and malaria are common.

A national social assistance program provides benefits for the elderly and persons with disabilities. All citizens beyond retirement age whose incomes fall below a minimum level are eligible for government pensions. There is free health care for pregnant women and children under six and free food for primary-school children in poor areas.

Malnutrition affects some 2.5 million children. It is especially common in former homelands and in urban

shantytowns (slums). Poverty, poor diet, and a lack of nutritional education are the main causes. Children who are malnourished are more susceptible to respiratory and other infections. Other health problems, such as tuberculosis, are also poverty related.

A long-standing housing shortage forces many poor families to live in overcrowded conditions, with an average of 2.3 persons per room. Many of these homes have no electricity and no running water. Waste disposal often consists of latrines—toilets that are simply holes in the

Squatter camps house hundreds of thousands of black South Africans. These camps are filled with shacks built with pieces of plastic, corrugated iron, and cardboard picked up from the dump.

Racially integrated classes, such as this one, are becoming commonplace in modern times.

ground. With such unsanitary conditions, diarrhea is common. A 2001 cholera epidemic in KwaZulu-Natal was partly due to floodwaters spreading human waste in villages. At least eight million South Africans have no access to clean drinking water. In poor rural areas, women have to haul water from distant sources.

Education

The South African government considers education a top priority. Under apartheid, schools were segregated. Schools for African children received little funding and lacked many basic needs. Schools for white children were generally well funded and provided a good education for their students.

Major reform began in 1993, when the government announced that education would be integrated. The reforms also acknowledged the need for communities to preserve their culture, religion, and language. When children started school in January 1995, all government-run primary and secondary schools were officially integrated. Yet the educational system remains segregated to a degree because many whites send their children to private schools, which few people from other population segments can afford.

Very few children attend preschool. Education is compulsory for all children between the ages of seven and sixteen. About 94 percent

Women have about the same literacy rate as men, but many girls drop out of high school because they are pregnant. A survey found that 20 percent of African women age 20 or over have no formal schooling, compared with 14 percent of African men.

of eligible students are enrolled in primary schools, and 51 percent attend secondary schools.

South Africa has more than 20,000 primary and secondary schools, including about 475 private schools. But the public system suffers from a lack of classrooms and qualified teachers. The national average is 1 teacher per 37 students. In some of the former homelands, there are between 48 and 100 pupils per classroom.

Most white and Asian students finish high school, and their literacy rates are high. African students have much less success in school and a lower literacy rate because of poverty-related factors and the scarcity of educational facilities in their communities. But colored students have the lowest levels of secondary school enrollment, while maintaining a high literacy rate.

The country has 21 universities and 139 technical colleges. Since the end of apartheid, more and more blacks are attending universities that were formerly set aside for white students.

Government studies indicate South Africa has an overall literacy rate of 82 percent for both males and females over the age of fifteen. Literacy is more common in urban centers, while illiteracy predominates in rural and poor communities.

Wits University, or the University of the Witwatersrand in Johannesburg, annually enrolls more than twenty thousand students. The school has had a nondiscrimination policy since it was founded more than eighty years ago. Many of its faculty members and students were banned from employment or jailed during apartheid for protesting its segregation laws.

CULTURAL LIFE

When apartheid ended, South Africa adopted the slogan the "Rainbow Nation," a reference to its efforts to blend its many different people into one nation. Indigenous African groups, the ancient Khoisan people, Afrikaners, people of British or Indian backgrounds, and new immigrants all contribute different elements to modern South Africa's cultural mix.

◉ Religion

The South African population is predominantly Christian. Almost 80 percent of South Africans, including 72 percent of blacks, practice this faith. The largest Christian church is Zion Christian Church, which flourishes in both urban and rural areas. The Dutch Reformed Church has about 3.8 million followers, and the Roman Catholic Church has at least 3.7 million members. Other Protestant religions, such as the Methodist, Anglican, and Lutheran churches, claim more than one million members each.

The Hindu religion dominates South Africa's Asian community, and the country also has a small Jewish community. Meanwhile, the number of South Africans who are Muslims (people who follow Islam) is growing. Immigrants from other African countries have recently converted many new believers in urban black communities. As yet, South Africa has few mosques (Islamic places of prayer), and many Muslims hold prayer services or after-school programs in their own homes.

Traditional African religions play an important role in many South Africans' spiritual lives. Many people comfortably combine traditional and Christian beliefs. While various ethnic groups have different traditions, most followers believe in a supreme being. Deceased ancestors are considered an important part of the community, providing a link with the spirit world and the powers that control everyday events. Angry ancestors can bring bad luck, so people keep their deceased relatives content with ritual offerings.

In her writings, **Nadine Gordimer** opposed her country's apartheid laws, in one instance calling the laws "clumsy words that reduced the delicacy and towering complexity of living to a race theory" (from *Occasion for Loving*, 1963).

Literature and Media

South Africa has produced a number of outstanding English-language writers. Nadine Gordimer, author of many fine works about South African society, received the 1991 Nobel Prize for Literature. Many contemporary authors, such as Andre Brink and Allister Sparks, focus on political and social themes in their novels. Alan Paton's *Cry, the Beloved Country* is a classic novel about apartheid. A number of South African writers, musicians, and other artists openly opposed apartheid, and some went into exile because of it.

Well-known black poets such as Mzwakhe Mbuli, sometimes known as the "people's poet," and Mongane Wally Serote also focus on the struggle against oppression. Nelson Mandela's autobiography *Long Walk to Freedom* became a popular seller around the world. Internationally acclaimed author J. M. Coetzee writes about his characters' interior struggles, while Wilbur Smith writes best-selling historical and adventure novels. New South African literary voices include Lesogo Rampolokeng, whose poetry is influenced by American rap music, and novelist Mark Behr.

A skillful San storyteller embellishes her story with dramatic gestures.

Indigenous African communities have a tradition of oral story-telling, proverbs, and family histories. On special occasions, presenters called *mbongi* perform *izibongo*—rhythmical, complex poems full of metaphors. Many of these stories have been written and preserved.

In Johannesburg the Market Theatre became famous when it continued to mount controversial plays during the apartheid years. Dramatist, actor, director, and novelist Athol Fugard has written several plays, including *My Children! My Africa!* about the tragedy of racial divisions. His work has been produced in New York and elsewhere. South Africa has not made a major impression internationally with its films, with the exception of the 1980 comedy *The Gods Must Be Crazy*. Its best-known film actor is Charlize Theron, who has appeared in a number of movies, including *The Legend of Bagger Vance*.

The South African Broadcasting Corporation, the country's public broadcaster, has nineteen radio stations with about twenty million

MARKET THEATRE

During the apartheid years, the Market Theatre defied the government by staging plays that protested government policies. It also allowed members of all ethnic groups to attend performances without the required permits. The theater in downtown Johannesburg opened in 1976 in a former market hall building. The building includes theaters, museums, and art galleries. Market Theatre still spotlights plays that comment on society, and it serves as a training ground for young actors and playwrights.

The television program *Isidingo* is South Africa's most popular soap opera, or "soapie." It has a multi-ethnic cast of characters and is set in a fictitious mining community called Horizon Deep. *Isidingo* explores the lives of community residents as they try to make sense of and survive the challenges facing the new South Africa. Their fight to ensure a future for the mine is pivotal to the story. Industrial espionage, fraud, murder, racism, and romance are intertwined in the plot.

listeners daily. It also has six television services broadcasting in eleven languages, two of which are pay channels distributed by satellite. About 85 percent of the country is within reach of a television signal. About half of broadcast television programs are produced in South Africa.

South Africa has about a dozen private radio stations broadcasting in various languages and more than eighty community radio stations. M-Net is a South African-based private television service that broadcasts a music video channel and other programming packages to subscribers across Africa.

The nation also has twenty-two daily newspapers and ten weekly newspapers, including three Sunday newspapers that can be considered national publications, as well as many small community newspapers. South African publishers also produce some three hundred consumer magazines.

If you'd like to learn more about South African culture, visit vgsbooks.com where you'll find links information on literature, music, and art, plus links to recipes and photograph.

Music

South Africans enjoy a wide variety of music. Favorites range from traditional African sounds and the Asian-influenced music of the Cape Malay community to jazz, rock, and classical. In some cases, these forms have blended. For example, some South African classical composers use traditional instruments—rattles, drums, and reed flutes—in their compositions. The San people even adapted their bows and arrows to make music.

Jazz, blues, and *kwela* music (simple saxophone-based jive tunes) were popular in the shebeens (informal bars) of the urban townships. Jazz remains extremely popular. Recent decades have seen a revival of *marabi* music, a product of the urban ghettos. Marabi features an improvisational style in which a solo vocalist is accompanied by an organ or an accordion. Young people also enjoy *kwaito,* a unique sound from the townships with repetitive lyrics influenced by protest chants. Internationally known South African musicians include singer Miriam Makeba, jazz trumpeter Hugh Masakela, the Zulu a cappella folk group Ladysmith Black Mambazo, Cape Town jazz stylist Abdullah Ibrahim, and reggae star Lucky Dube. Some of these musicians became familiar around the world when they lived abroad during apartheid.

South Africans love to sing choral music, and school and adult choirs compete for awards. The largest cities have their own symphony orchestras or chamber music groups, such as the Soweto String Quartet. Many people attend outdoor classical concerts on summer evenings.

On the way to a **choir rehearsal** in the Eastern Cape province, three women warm up their voices by singing a Xhosa-language hymn.

This **Zulu beaded figure** has a mealie-cob (corncob) inside its body.

Art and Architecture

Some of the earliest artworks in the world were drawn and engraved on flat rocks and boulders in South Africa. Some of these drawings may be twenty-five thousand to ten thousand years old. Others were done more recently by the San people. Found mainly in the arid interior plains and in the Drakensberg and Cedarberg Mountains, the images represent a range of subjects, including hunting and rainmaking.

Indigenous crafts include beadwork jewelry, baskets made of woven grasses, and pots made from rolled coils of clay. Carved and painted wooden ceremonial masks are sold to collectors, while daily utensils such as spoons are often carved from a single piece of wood. Weavers combine tiny colored beads in geometric patterns. The glass beads, introduced by traders in the 1800s, came to indicate the status and ethnic affiliation of the wearer, while the colors symbolize messages such as love and faithfulness. Since 1994 the government has built several cultural villages in which traditional crafts are demonstrated to visitors.

MAPUNGUBWE

More and more South Africans are recognizing the significance of their African cultural heritage. For example, a permanent exhibition opened at the University of Pretoria in 2000. On display were sophisticated objects from Mapungubwe, an archaeological site dating from about A.D. 1000 to 1300. This site on a hilltop near the Limpopo River was discovered in the 1930s. Artifacts include a gold rhinoceros and other gold ornaments, pottery, and ceramic figures.

Well-known South African artists include pioneer painter Irma Stern and William Kentridge, a contemporary artist and animated filmmaker. Black artists have not had the same access to training as whites, although several arts centers have been established since the 1960s to offer art education. A number of black visual artists, including sculptor Ezrom Legae, have achieved international recognition, by blending traditional and Western influences.

South African architecture varies between regions, depending on available materials and ethnic and historical influences. Houses in the Cape region are famous for their unique Cape Dutch style, which is characterized by whitewashed walls, decorative structural features, and shuttered windows. In the Karoo region, the Cape Dutch style became a flat-roofed house with a *stoep* (porch) or veranda.

In Port Elizabeth and Grahamstown, houses with elegant terraces were influenced by British architecture, while Pietermaritzburg is known for its Victorian-style brick homes. Durban buildings also show British influences, while the city's Hindu temples reflect Indian traditions.

Downtown Johannesburg features stark office towers of steel and glass built by well-known South African architects such as Helmut Jahn. The Reserve Bank headquarters in Pretoria is the tallest building in Africa. Many Dutch Reform churches are similarly modern in design and are built of brick and steel.

This **church in Fauresmith** *(above)* is an example of a modern design, while **Groot Constantia** *(left)*, a museum in modern times, was built in the Cape Dutch style as a residence on one of the first European estates in South Africa.

This distinctive, older **Ndebele home** is painted in traditional geometric designs and in muted earth tones. In modern times, the preferred colors have changed to bright reds, purples, yellows, and blues.

Township suburbs have row upon row of rectangular matchbox houses, so called because they are so small. They are usually built of cement, concrete blocks, or of corrugated iron sheets. Traditional round houses called *rondavels* still exist in a few regions. The Zulu beehive home, made of saplings and woven grass, has all but disappeared. The Ndebele people like to paint the outside walls of their homes with colorful geometric decorations.

Food

South Africans enjoy a vast array of flavors, from hot curries to fresh seafood and sweets. Culinary influences arrived over time from other parts of Africa, from Asia, and from Europe.

Game meat, such as impala and springbok, is popular, as well as beef and lamb. Most South Africans enjoy a *braaie*—a barbeque of grilled meat or seafood. During the Great Trek, the Afrikaners prepared meat with salt and spices before drying and slicing it. Such dried meat, called *biltong,* is still popular. Afrikaner traditional cooking includes stews and cakes flavored with cinnamon, anise, and other spices.

The Malay slaves who arrived in the late 1600s had a profound influence on cooking, especially in the Cape. They used spices such as fennel and ginger, as well as saltpeter, which is used for pickling. Pickled fish is a staple of Cape Malay cooking. *Bobotie,* a curried meatloaf flavored with chutney (a thick fruit sauce), is another popular dish.

The food found in Indian homes and restaurants is spicier than that of the Cape Malay. Both Malay and Indian cooks serve roti, or unleavened bread, and samosas, small pastries filled with spicy meat or vegetables. The French Huguenots planted sturdy vines and developed excellent wines. They also made pastries, fruit preserves in syrup, and bread rolls called *mosbolletjies.* People dry the bread rolls in the oven to enjoy with coffee in the morning.

BOBOTIE

2 medium onions, chopped

2 pounds ground lamb or beef

1 tablespoon olive oil

1 slice bread torn into pieces

1½ cups milk

2 teaspoons curry powder

salt and pepper, to taste

2 tablespoons fruit chutney

1 teaspoon brown sugar

6 bay leaves

¼ cup currants or golden raisins

6 almonds, quartered

2 beaten eggs

1. Preheat oven to 350°F.
2. In a frying pan, brown the onions and meat in olive oil. Pour off excess fat.
3. Soak the bread in ½ cup milk.
4. In a greased 1½-quart casserole dish, place the meat, bread mixture, curry powder, salt and pepper, chutney, brown sugar, bay leaves, currants, and almonds.
5. Combine the remaining milk with the beaten eggs and pour over the top.
6. Bake for 35 minutes, or until the custard has set.
7. Serve with steamed rice or couscous. Sliced banana, fresh vegetables, or green salad also taste great with bobotie.

Serves 6

Pap, or porridge made from ground maize (corn), is a traditional African breakfast favorite. Beans, stewed pumpkin, peanuts, *maas* (sour milk), and *phutu pap* (crumbly porridge) are also African staples.

Sports

With good weather year-round, South Africa is a sports lover's paradise. Among the most popular sports are soccer, rugby, cricket, golf, boxing, tennis, and cycling. Water sports such as sailing and canoeing are popular. Durban is South Africa's surfing capital.

Soccer, called football in South Africa, is the nation's number one sport. The national team, Bafana Bafana (Zulu for "The Boys, The Boys") reached the finals of the World Cup in 1998. Rugby (a game similar to American football) is also popular, and the national team, the Springboks, snatched the world championship in 1995.

For many years, South African athletes did not engage in international competition. South Africa was banned from the Olympics in 1960 due to the racial segregation of its sports teams. Until recently,

Local soccer teams face off at Hout Bay and draw a crowd.

sports programs in black communities also suffered from a lack of funding, facilities, and equipment.

Well-known sports figures include golfers Gary Player and Ernie Els, boxer Baby Jake Matlala, soccer star Sibusiso Zuma, and swimmer Penny Heyns. Since returning to international competition, South Africans have taken Olympic medals in swimming and track and field.

Holidays

South Africa's holiday calendar includes the usual celebrations, such as New Year's Day and Christmas Day. The day after Christmas is called Goodwill Day. Family Day is celebrated in April, and May 1 is celebrated as Workers' Day.

Since 1994 several public holidays have been added or renamed. Human Rights Day, which falls on March 21, recognizes the importance of the Bill of Rights, a cornerstone of democracy in South Africa. It commemorates March 21, 1960, when at least 67 demonstrators were killed and 186 wounded by police in Sharpeville during a protest against the pass laws.

April 27, Freedom Day, commemorates the first democratic elections in South Africa. June 16 is Youth Day, honoring the student uprising in Soweto. August 9, National Women's Day, commemorates the day in 1956 when women participated in a march against the pass laws. September 24, Heritage Day, celebrates South Africa's ethnicity, creative expression, language, and food and promotes the idea that diversity brings strength, not conflict. Each year a different theme is emphasized.

December 16 is the Day of Reconciliation. On this date in 1838, thousands of Zulu warriors attacked a group of about 470 Voortrekkers. The Voortrekkers vowed they would build a church if they won the battle. With the advantage they had of guns over Zulu spears, they killed several thousand Zulu, while only three Voortrekkers were wounded. For many years, Afrikaners celebrated December 16 as the Day of the Vow. But since the end of apartheid, this national holiday carries the spirit of national reconciliation and unity.

South Africans also hold local and regional festivals all year long. In September several towns organize festivals to celebrate the spring wildflowers. Christmas means summer holidays for the children, and industries also shut down for several weeks. Some families head for the beach. Many black families pile into crowded buses and travel to the villages where they grew up or have relatives. In the summer, outdoor concerts, open-air theater performances, and sporting events are popular. Autumn brings agricultural shows. During winter marathon races and canoeing events take place.

At an **Afrikaner festival,** dancers demonstrate folk dances for diners.

THE ECONOMY

South Africa has the largest and best-developed economy in sub-Saharan Africa, but the international economic sanctions imposed to protest apartheid seriously damaged the country's economy. Yet with the arrival of democracy, many foreign governments have tried to encourage South Africa by providing economic assistance. In 1994 the ANC government designed a Reconstruction and Development Program that would bring clean water, housing, and electricity to millions of people. But the country was deeply in debt, and the government opted for a conservative economic strategy that would keep expenses low and help it to reduce the budget deficit. The country's long-term recovery plan emphasized controlled spending.

By the early 2000s, the government had made slow progress on several fronts. Since 1994, 1.2 million new houses had been constructed. Seven million more people had access to piped water, and 3.5 million had acquired access to electricity. But a report by Statistics South Africa indicated that, at the same time, the number of unemployed

South Africans had increased by 50 percent. This was because the economy failed to create enough jobs to keep up with population growth. Blacks were especially hard hit by unemployment.

Although analysts have said the economy is basically healthy, the national currency, the rand, declined in the years after apartheid. In 2001 it lost more than 30 percent of its value. Businesses, including those from the United Kingdom, the country's biggest foreign investor, avoided major investments in South Africa, and several large companies moved their headquarters from Johannesburg to London.

Many current economic problems, including high poverty and unemployment levels among blacks, are a result of apartheid. When white leaders gave up political power at the end of apartheid, they did not give up economic power. Whites have largely retained control of businesses, industries, and land. The lack of education and training for blacks during apartheid has hurt the economy. Black workers with the training required to fill skilled jobs remain in short supply.

Receptionists keep Microsoft's Johannesburg office running smoothly.

Black empowerment programs are helping blacks to advance in large corporations, in civil service, and to gain experience in running businesses. But a large gap remains between middle-class, educated blacks and the majority of blacks, who remain poor.

At one time, South Africa's economy was primarily based on mining and agriculture. But in recent decades, manufacturing and services have become greater contributors to the gross domestic product (GDP, or the value of production within the country's borders by citizens and noncitizens). Still, mining remains important, as gold accounts for more than one-third of exports, and agriculture creates many jobs.

The World Bank valued South Africa's GDP at $126 billion in 2000. It was then growing at an annual rate of 3 percent. Average per capita income was equivalent to $3,020, placing South Africa among the world's middle-income countries. Income disparities, however, are among the most extreme in the world. While some South Africans enjoy a high standard of living, millions live in abject poverty. In the early 2000s, more than half of South Africans lived on less than $82 a month.

Services and Industry

The largest sector of the formal economy is the service sector. It contributes 66 percent of GDP and employs 54 percent of the employed labor force in government offices, schools, hotels, stores, and restaurants. Because the country has so much to offer visitors, the tourism industry is booming. Many banks and insurance companies operate throughout the country, and a stock exchange exists in Johannesburg.

The craftsperson offering **this Ndeble beadwork** for sale *(left)* is part of the informal sector of the South African economy. It is a growing source of employment, especially for blacks. According to government estimates, at least 1.7 million people work in occupations such as craft making, street vending, domestic work, repairing vehicles, or house painting.

Industry is the second largest sector, representing 31 percent of GDP and employing 25 percent of the workforce in mining, manufacturing, construction, and power production. Manufacturing contributes 19 percent of GDP, and 14 percent of workers are employed making iron and steel, chemicals, petroleum, coal products, food products, transport equipment, machinery, paper, and textiles. Most industries are located in large urban centers such as Johannesburg, Cape Town, Port Elizabeth, and Durban.

South Africa is famous for its diamonds and remains the world's leading producer of gold. Its mines also produce iron ore, coal, platinum, chromium, and other minerals. Much of South Africa's mineral wealth is exported. The mining

The rand, the South African currency, is not to be confused with the Krugerrand. The Krugerrand is a gold coin, consisting of a certain weight of pure gold and with no face value. It was first introduced by the South African Chamber of Mines in 1967 as a way to market gold to coin collectors. Most people who buy gold as a financial investment purchase it as Krugerrands.

South Africa's national energy company is experimenting with solar energy—a power source that could supplement or replace dirty, inefficient coal. The company is installing solar panels in some homes. This power source could be useful to the 20 percent of rural homes that are not expected to have access to the country's electricity system for many years.

industry contributes about 6 percent of GDP and provides jobs for almost 5 percent of the formal workforce.

The government-owned power company Eskom supplies energy. Some 90 percent of South Africa's electricity comes from coal-burning electric power stations. Energy is also produced by a nuclear power station and by hydroelectric sources. Hydroelectric power is also imported from Lesotho and Mozambique.

Agriculture, Fishing, and Forestry

Agriculture, fishing, and forestry together contribute 4 percent of GDP and engage 11 percent of the employed workforce. Maize is the dietary staple of most South Africans. Other important crops include wheat, sorghum, peanuts, and soybeans. South Africa is one of the world's largest producers of sugarcane. Farmers also grow grapes and fruit, including pears, peaches, bananas, and oranges. Cattle and sheep are raised for meat, dairy products, and wool.

The commercial fishing industry, located primarily on the western and southern coasts, brings in squid, oysters, and rock lobsters. Commercial fish species include anchovies, herring, sole, and tuna.

South Africa has developed one of the world's largest artificial forest industries. Pine, eucalyptus, and wattle are grown on plantations to produce wood for pulp and paper products, mining timbers, and other products. Wood is the major source of fuel for about twelve million South Africans.

Workers load sugarcane in railroad cars. A train will carry it to distant markets.

Land reform has become a crucial issue since the end of apartheid. Laws passed in 1913 and 1936 made it illegal for black Africans to buy land outside designated reserves. After 1948 and accelerating through the 1960s, more than four million black South Africans were forced to leave their land and sell their cattle at a fraction of their value. Commercial white farmers and industries needed blacks to work as low-wage laborers, rather than on their own subsistence farms.

When the ANC came to power in 1994, whites owned most of the fertile land and had mechanized farms. Blacks were crowded into infertile regions. The government has set up a program to help people buy the land at fair value from willing sellers. A group of low-income households can jointly apply for a land purchase grant. More than one million acres (400,000 hectares) of land has been redistributed. But it may take many years before the land reform process is complete.

Transportation

With no navigable rivers, South Africa's rail, road, and air transportation systems are crucial. A total of about 331,890 miles (534,130 km) of roads serve the nation. Two-lane roads connect most towns, and a four-lane highway connects Johannesburg and Durban. Tolls on some roads raise funds for maintenance, but many roads (as well as railway and port facilities) are in poor condition.

Railways have been the backbone of South Africa's transportation network since the first track was built in the 1870s. The modern rail

These **giraffes get a ride** on a modern highway.

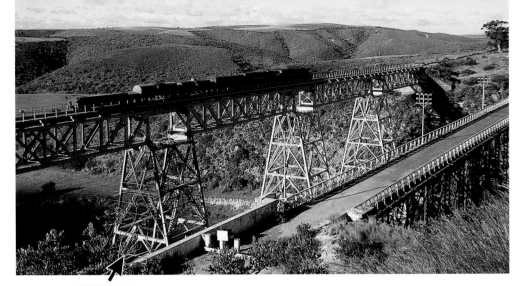
A **freight train** crosses a rural trestle (bridge).

system serves most cities, towns, and rural areas. Luxury passenger service exists on the 1,000-mile (1,600-km) route between Pretoria, Johannesburg, and Cape Town. Most trains carry freight, especially coal, minerals, and agricultural products. The majority of locomotives are powered by electricity.

Air service operates between all major cities and between South Africa and major centers around the world. Johannesburg, Durban, and Cape Town are the main airports. Durban is the main seaport, while Port Elizabeth, Cape Town, and East London provide port services to their regions. Richards Bay in KwaZulu-Natal is primarily a coal-exporting port, and Saldanha Bay, north of Cape Town, is an iron shipment center.

Trade

South Africa's main trading partners are Great Britain, the United States, Germany, and Japan. The country exports iron, steel and other mining products, transportation equipment, food, and chemical products. It imports vehicles and auto parts, industrial machinery, chemical products, and petroleum.

South Africa is a member of the Southern African Development Community (SADC), a fourteen-country organization that encourages economic development, peace, and security in the region. South Africa is also part of the African Development Bank, which has seventy-seven member countries from Africa, North and South America, Europe, and Asia and promotes economic and social development in Africa through loans, investments, and technical assistance. President Mbeki is a guiding force behind the New Partnership for Africa's Development (NEPAD), an organization designed to develop African economies. It seeks to bring aid, trade, and investment to African nations that make democratic reforms.

The Future

In many ways, South Africa's future looks promising. The nation pulled off an amazing feat by eliminating an oppressive political system without full-scale civil war. It has solid institutions and a large population, some of whom are experienced union, business, and political leaders. The country is highly industrialized and rich in resources. South Africa's democratic institutions seem strong, although the political scales are heavily balanced on the ANC's side. Racism, although still present, is no longer a dominant factor.

Serious problems remain, however, including government debt and the need for better housing, education, and health services. Crime poses a major threat to economic development because it scares off investors and pushes skilled and educated people to leave.

Apartheid affected almost every part of South African life, and many people still bear the scars of this system. Nevertheless, Nelson Mandela has called forgiveness a patriotic duty. Although South Africa has become a much more equitable nation politically, the economic situation is still divided along racial lines. Blacks suffer from poverty, and whites are relatively well off. As Mandela admitted, South Africans have only taken the first steps of a long and difficult journey.

Sprinklers at a Cape Town nursery invite **two friends** to dash through the spray.

CA. 117,000 B.C   *Homo sapiens* leave footprints at Langebaan Lagoon.

CA. A.D. 200   Sheep are herded extensively in the Cape Peninsula region.

CA. 1000   Mixed farming and small villages are established throughout eastern South Africa by Bantu-speaking people.

1497   Vasco da Gama finds a route from Europe to India via the Cape of Good Hope.

1652   Jan van Riebeeck establishes a refreshment station at Table Bay (modern Cape Town).

1795   Britain takes the colony from the Dutch.

1816   Shaka creates a Zulu kingdom. A twelve-year period of warfare and famine, known as the *mfecane*, begins.

1820   The first large group of British settlers arrive.

1834   Voortrekkers leave Cape Colony to begin the Great Trek.

1838   The Voortrekkers defeat Zulu attackers at Blood River.

C.A. 1860   Indian contract laborers arrive to work on sugarcane plantations.

1867   Diamonds are discovered in South Africa.

1886   Gold is discovered on the Witwatersrand.

1892   A railroad between Cape Colony ports and the Witwatersrand mining and industrial area is completed.

1899   The Afrikaaners declare war on the British, beginning the Boer War.

1902   A peace treaty is signed, ending the Boer War.

1910   Louis Botha becomes the first prime minister of the Union of South Africa.

1912   The South African Native National Congress, which later becomes the African National Congress (ANC), is founded.

1913   The Natives Land Act prohibits Africans from buying or renting land outside the reserves from people who are not Africans.

1948   Alan Paton's novel *Cry, the Beloved Country* is published.

1950   The National Party government passes the Population Registration Act, which classifies every South African by race.

1960   Police kill 67 people and wound 186 demonstrating against the pass laws in Sharpeville.

1961   South Africa withdraws from the Commonwealth and becomes a republic.

1964   Nelson Mandela and other ANC leaders are sentenced to life imprisonment for treason.

1966   Prime Minister Verwoerd is assassinated by a deranged parliamentary messenger.

1967   Dr. Christiaan Barnard performs the world's first human heart transplant in Cape Town.

1973   The United Nations declares apartheid a crime against humanity.

1976   Soweto schoolchildren protest against South Africa's pass laws.

1984   Bishop Desmond Tutu is awarded the Nobel Peace Prize for leading nonviolent protests against apartheid.

1990   President F. W. de Klerk lifts the ban on the ANC and releases Nelson Mandela from prison. Nadine Gordimer wins the Nobel Prize for Literature.

1993   Nelson Mandela and F. W. de Klerk share the Nobel Peace Prize.

1994   Multiracial election takes place. Mandela is elected president.

1995   The Springboks, South Africa's national rugby team, wins the World Cup.

1996   Truth and Reconciliation Commission hearings begin.

1999   The ANC is returned to power in national elections. Thabo Mbeki becomes president.

2002   The UN-sponsored World Summit on Sustainable Development is held in Johannesburg.

2003   President Mbeki announces "black economic empowerment" proposals designed to help black South Africans set up their own businesses.

COUNTRY NAME Republic of South Africa

AREA 472,856 square miles (1,224,692 sq. km)

MAIN LANDFORMS Plateau, Coastal Strip, Cape Mountains Region, Namib Desert, Kalahari Desert

HIGHEST POINT Champagne Castle 11,072 ft (3,375 m) above sea level

LOWEST POINT Sea level

MAJOR RIVERS Orange River, Vaal River, Limpopo River

ANIMALS Lion, elephant, rhinoceros, springbok, meerkat, African hoopoe, coelacanth, Cape rock lobster

CAPITAL CITY Cape Town (legislative), Pretoria (administrative), Bloemfontein (judicial)

OTHER MAJOR CITIES Johannesburg, Durban, Port Elizabeth

OFFICIAL LANGUAGES Zulu, Xhosa, Afrikaans, Pedi, English, Tswana, Sotho, Tsonga, Swazi, Venda, Ndebele

MONETARY UNIT Rand. 100 cents=1 rand.

SOUTH AFRICAN CURRENCY

The South African currency is the rand, a shortened form of the Afrikaans word "Witwatersrand." This currency replaced the pound in 1961, when South Africa became a republic. Coins are found in 5-rand, 2-rand, 1-rand, 50-cent, 20-cent, 5-cent, 2-cent, and 1-cent denominations. Paper notes come in R200, R100, R50, R20, and R10 denominations, each in a different color and illustrated with a different wild animal.

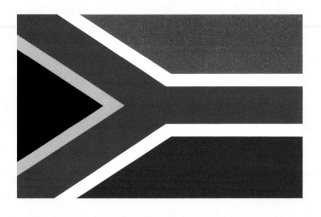

The national flag was flown for the first time on Freedom Day, April 27, 1994. The flag, designed by F. Brownell, consists of a green Y, bordered top and bottom in white, extending from the upper and lower left-hand corners, converging and flowing as a single horizontal band toward the other edge. This symbolizes the convergence of diverse elements in South African society, taking the road ahead in unity. Above and below the Y are bands of red and blue, respectively. Inside the triangle made by the top of the Y is a band of golden yellow and a black triangle. The red, white, and blue are the colors of the old South African flag, while the black, gold, and green are the colors of the ANC.

The national anthem, chosen in 1996, combines shortened versions of two anthems, "Nkosi sikelel' iAfrika" and "Die Stem van Suid-Afrika/ The Call of South Africa." The first two verses are in Xhosa and set to one tune. Then the melody changes, and the last verses are in Afrikaans and English. "Nkosi sikelel' iAfrika" was composed as a hymn in 1897 by a schoolteacher, Enoch Sontonga. Additional stanzas in Xhosa were later added by the poet Samuel Mqhayi. Eventually, the hymn became a political protest anthem.

"Die Stem van Suid-Afrika" is a poem written by C. J. Langenhoven in 1918. The music was composed by the Reverend M. L. de Villiers in 1921. It was played along with the British national anthem, "God Save the King," every day on radio for many years before the government made it the official anthem in 1957. The official English version, "The Call of South Africa," was accepted in 1952.

**"Nkosi sikelel' iAfrika and
Die Stem van Suid-Afrika/The Call of South Africa"**
Sound the call to come together,
And united we shall stand,
Let us live and strive for freedom,
In South Africa our land.

For a link where you can hear South Africa's national anthem, go to vgsbooks.com.

FREDERIK WILLEM DE KLERK (b. 1936) The son of a prominent Afrikaner politician, de Klerk was born in Johannesburg. A lawyer, de Klerk joined the National Party and was elected to Parliament in 1972. In 1989 he became president of South Africa. He negotiated a peaceful end to apartheid and the creation of a democratic constitution and nonracial society. He was deputy president under Mandela, then leader of the opposition until his retirement in 1997.

ERNIE ELS (b. 1969) Born in Johannesburg, Els started playing golf at age nine. He has been one of the world's best golfers since his professional debut in 1989. He has twice won the prestigious U.S. Open golf championship and has won more than two dozen tournaments around the world. Els had made numerous contributions to charitable causes, and his Ernie Els Foundation is dedicated to helping disadvantaged children.

NADINE GORDIMER (b. 1923) The award-winning writer grew up in a middle-class Russian immigrant family in a town near Johannesburg. Most of her unsentimental novels and short stories revolve around themes of politics, alienation, and the impact of apartheid on the lives of individuals. She has written ten novels and several collections of short stories. Along with other international honors, she won the Nobel Prize for Literature in 1991.

WINNIE MADIKIZELA-MANDELA (b. 1934) A social worker born in Bizana, Eastern Cape, Winnie Madikizela married Nelson Mandela in 1958. After he was imprisoned, she was also banned from political activity but became a popular anti-apartheid activist. In 1988 she and her bodyguards were linked to the kidnapping of four youths, one of whom was murdered, and she was eventually found guilty of kidnapping. In 1993 she was elected president of the ANC Women's League. She served as a government minister until Mandela removed her for publicly criticizing the government. They were divorced in 1996.

MIRIAM MAKEBA (b. 1932) The singer known as Mama Africa was born in a township near Johannesburg. When she was 20, she began singing with a popular local jazz group. Her appearance in a documentary movie brought her international attention, and she began to perform with American singer Harry Belafonte. In 1960 the South African government banned her because of her outspoken opposition to apartheid, and she spent thirty years in exile.

NELSON MANDELA (b. 1918) The son of a chief of the Xhosa-speaking Tembu people, Mandela—or Madiba, as he is sometimes called—was born in the small village of Mvezo, Eastern Cape. He was educated at a mission school and earned his law degree in 1942. He joined the ANC two years later. Tried for treason in 1964, he was sentenced to life imprisonment. From prison he worked to negotiate an end to apartheid. Released in 1990, he shared the Nobel Peace Prize with F. W. de Klerk in 1993 and became president of South Africa in 1994. He retired in 1999.

THABO MBEKI (b. 1942) Born in Idutywa, Eastern Cape, Mbeki joined the ANC Youth League in 1956. In the late 1960s, Mbeki trained as a guerrilla fighter in Russia. He advanced within the ANC and played an important role in negotiating the agreement that ended apartheid. In 1997 he succeeded Mandela as president of the ANC, and in 1999, he became president of South Africa.

GARY PLAYER (b. 1935) Player is one of the greatest golfers of all time. Born in Johannesburg, Player turned professional at age eighteen and is one of only five players to win each of the major golf championships—the Masters, the U.S. Open, the British Open, and the PGA Championship—winning a total of nine of these events. His career golf winnings have totaled more than $10 million, and Player has given a large percentage of his earnings to the Player Foundation, an organization committed to improving schools in South Africa.

SHAKA (ca. 1787–1828) This Zulu warrior became chief of a small Zulu clan in about 1816. He reorganized the clan's army, gave his warriors short spears for close combat, and devised a strong battlefield formation. By the 1820s, the Zulus had become a militarized society and controlled a large territory between the Great Escarpment and the sea, north of the Tugela River. The raids Shaka ordered killed thousands of civilians and devastated Natal. Survivors who had not been absorbed by the Zulus led their own raids into the interior, as they searched for new land. Shaka was assassinated in 1828.

CHARLIZE THERON (b. 1975) Theron, a well-known actress, was born in Benoni, a small town outside of Johannesburg. She grew up in an Afrikaner family and began her performance career as a professional dancer at age six. When a knee injury ended her dancing career, she moved on to acting in the mid-1990s. She has appeared in numerous films, including *That Thing You Do!, The Devil's Advocate, The Legend of Bagger Vance, Sweet November*, and *The Italian Job*.

DESMOND TUTU (b. 1931) Born in Klerksdorp, North West province, Tutu was educated in mission schools and became a teacher in 1954. Later, Tutu studied theology and was ordained an Anglican priest in 1960. He became the first black secretary-general of the South African Council of Churches in 1978 and first black archbishop of Cape Town in 1986. This position made him the head of the Anglican Church in South Africa. He championed nonviolent protest against apartheid and was awarded the Nobel Peace Prize in 1984. In 1996 he chaired the Truth and Reconciliation Commission.

APARTHEID MUSEUM The Apartheid Museum, opened in 2001 near Johannesburg, gives visitors a taste of what living under apartheid was like. At the entrance, visitors are randomly assigned a skin color and told to enter either by the door for whites or the door for nonwhites. Exhibits include passbooks and identity cards, street signs indicating restricted areas, nooses hanging from the ceiling along with the names of political prisoners who were executed, and film clips of speeches, riots, and brutality.

CAPE TOWN Cape Town is one of Africa's most beautiful cities. Visitors to the city can take a short trip to Table Mountain, where they can enjoy hiking, cable car rides, and rock climbing. The Victoria and Alfred Waterfront area offers a variety of fun diversions, including boat trips, shopping, street musicians, and museums. Cape Point, located south of the city, features a colorful array of unique plants and animals, including more than 150 different species of birds.

KRUGER NATIONAL PARK This refuge for wildlife includes lions, elephants, zebras, baboons, and giraffes. The 7,580-square-mile (19,633-sq.-km) area of Bushveld is the size of Israel. The park was named after Paul Kruger, president of the South African Republic from 1883 to 1900. Its various habitats are home to about 100 species of reptiles, 430 species of birds, and 140 species of mammals.

NAMAQUALAND This 18,500-square-mile (47,900-sq.-km) region on the arid west coast is famous for its spectacular floral displays. In spring (August to October), if the rains have been sufficient, the plain bursts into bloom and on sunny days is covered by a carpet of flowers. More than four thousand floral species are found in this region, but most are a type of succulent daisy.

ROBBEN ISLAND This low-lying island in the cold Atlantic near Cape Town became famous as the prison that held Nelson Mandela and several other anti-apartheid leaders for many years. It was first used as a prison in 1636 and held other political prisoners in the 1800s.

STERKFONTEIN CAVES These caves and other nearby fossil sites are the source of a rich trove of fossils, including Mrs. Ples, and a 3.3 million-year-old complete hominid skeleton called Little Foot. In all, the area has produced about five hundred hominid fossils and nine-thousand stone tools.

VOORTREKKER MONUMENT This Pretoria monument was built in memory of the Voortrekkers who left the Cape Colony to escape British rule in the 1830s. Construction of the monument began in 1938, the one hundredth anniversary of the Battle of Blood River, in which the Boers defeated the Zulus. The memorial became a symbol of Afrikaner nationalism.

Afrikaans: a simplified form of Dutch that has dropped certain sounds and words and incorporated new words from other languages. Afrikaans originated as a spoken language used by the Dutch and the slaves but became increasingly common in the 1700s.

apartheid: a policy of segregation and political and economic discrimination against nonwhites in the Republic of South Africa

Bantu: a family of languages spoken in central and southern Africa; a member of any group of African peoples who speak these languages

embargo: the prohibition of trade or arms shipments

Kaffir: a name used by Europeans to refer to African mixed-race farmers. This term later came to be a derogatory name for black Africans.

maize: another name for corn, which South Africans also call mealie. Native to the Americas, it was introduced to southern Africa by the Portuguese.

migrant labor: in South Africa, an economic system in which the children would live in the family's home village with the mother or other relatives, while the father and/or mother would move to the city or mines to work

paleontology: a science dealing with past geological periods as known through fossil remains

pass laws: laws in existence from the 1940s until 1991 that required black people to carry identifying papers, or passes, and that restricted their freedom to move in areas designated for whites only, unless they were employed there

shebeen: an often unlicensed bar in a black township where liquor, sometimes home brewed, is sold

succulent: a plant with fleshy tissues that conserve water

township: an area in South Africa, usually close to a large urban center, segregated for occupation by persons of non-European descent. Although South Africa has been officially desegregated, most blacks continue to live in these communities.

veld: an Afrikaans word meaning "rolling grassland"

Glossary

Byrnes, Rita M., ed. *South Africa: A Country Study.* **Washington, D.C.: Library of Congress Federal Research Division, 1997.**
This helpful volume in the Library of Congress's Area Handbook Series provides accurate information on South Africa's geography, history, people, and economy.

De Villers, et al. *Insight Guide: South Africa.* **London: APA Publications, 1999.**
This well-illustrated guidebook is a great introduction to the people, flora and fauna, and places of South Africa.

EIA South Africa. **September 2, 2002.**
Website: <http://www.eia.doe.gov/emeu/cabs/safrica.html> (May 6, 2003).
This website presents an analysis prepared by the U.S. government's Energy Information Administration. It focuses on energy use and environmental issues in South Africa.

Europa Publications. *Europa World Yearbook 2002.* **London: Europa Publications, 2001.**
This annual guide focuses on recent political events and has a variety of economic and other statistics on South Africa and many other countries.

Goodman, David. *Fault Lines: Journeys into the New South Africa.* **Berkeley, CA: University of California Press, 1999.**
In this revealing account, a journalist visits a white farmer, a black businesswoman, and others to see how much South African society has really changed since the end of apartheid.

Krog, Antjie. *Country of My Skull: Guilt, Sorrow, and the Limits of Forgiveness in the New South Africa.* **New York: Three Rivers Press, 1998.**
This disturbing but eloquently written book focuses on the Truth and Reconciliation Commission. It explores the nature of evil, truth, guilt, and forgiveness.

Population Reference Bureau. **February 13, 2002.**
Website: <http://www.prb.org> (May 6, 2003).
This is a reliable site for statistics on world population trends. Visit this site to find a fact sheet on South Africa's health and population statistics.

Reader, John. *Africa: A Biography of the Continent.* **London: Penguin Books, 1998.**
Anyone who is interested in Africa will enjoy this highly readable book. It puts South African history in the context of developments across the continent.

Sampson, Anthony. *Mandela: The Authorised Biography.* **London: HarperCollins, 1999.**
This biography describes the life of the South African leader.

South Africa Government Online. **May 5, 2003.**
Website: <http://www.gov.za/> (May 5, 2003).
This government website is extensive, easy to navigate, and continuously updated. The section called "SA: An Overview" contains articles on South

Africa's population and physical features, public holidays, national symbols, natural resources, and social services.

Thompson, Leonard. *A History of South Africa*. Rev. ed. New Haven, CT: Yale University Press, 1995.
This history of South Africa is a standard reference work. It seeks to balance the perspectives of both blacks and whites and to give an accurate portrayal of the nation's history from prehistoric times to the election of the ANC in 1994.

Turner, Barry, ed. *The Statesman's Yearbook: The Politics, Cultures and Economies of the World, 2002*. New York: Macmillan Press, 2001.
This is a good source for statistical and background information on countries of the world, including South Africa.

Waldmeir, Patti. *Anatomy of a Miracle: The End of Apartheid and the Birth of the New South Africa*. New York: W. W. Norton and Company, 1997.
This is a fascinating account of the events and behind-the-scenes negotiations that allowed apartheid to die, the ruling National Party to give up power, and a new South African government to be elected in 1994.

Encounter South Africa.
Website: <http://www.encounter.co.za/> **(May 6, 2003)**
This on-line travel magazine is updated daily. It features articles on wildlife, cultural villages, South Africa's World Heritage Sites, and other topics that will take you on an armchair tour of this beautiful country.

Finlayson, Reggie. *Nelson Mandela.* **Minneapolis: Lerner Publications Company, 1999.**
This is a biography of South Africa's leader in the struggle against apartheid and of its first black president.

Frontline: The Long Walk of Nelson Mandela
Website: <http://www.pbs.org/wgbh/pages/frontline/shows/mandela/> **(May 6, 2003)**
This website, designed to accompany a PBS documentary, includes interviews with friends and excerpts from Mandela's autobiography, *Long Walk to Freedom.*

Gleimius, Nita, Evelina Sibanyoni, and Emma Mthimunye. *The Zulu of Africa.* **Minneapolis: Lerner Publications Company, 2003.**
This book profiles the Zulu of South Africa, describing their history, culture, religion, family life, language, economy, and their struggle to maintain cultural traditions in the modern world.

Gordimer, Nadine. *Jump and Other Stories.* **London: Penguin Books, 1991.**
Politics is the thread that binds this collection of short stories by the Nobel prize-winning author. Characters include a political activist in hiding and a white suburbanite who stumbles into a black shantytown.

Kruger, Kobie. *The Wilderness Family: At Home with Africa's Wildlife.* **New York: Ballantine Books, 2001.**
The author, her game warden husband, and children spent seventeen years living in Kruger National Park. This account describes her adventures and observations of assorted animals and visitors.

Martin, Christopher. *Mohandas Ganhdi.* **Minneapolis: Lerner Publications Company, 2001.**
This is a biography of the Indian lawyer, who experienced racial injustice during his time living in South Africa.

Mathabane, Mark. *Kaffir Boy: An Autobiography.* **New York: Touchstone, 1986.**
As Mark Mathabane grew up in a poor family in a Johannesburg township, he and his family experienced starvation, humiliation, and finally hope. Mathabane was smart and athletic and got a lucky break that allowed him to leave his country, but millions of others remained behind.

McCord, Margaret. *The Calling of Katie Makanya: A Memoir of South Africa.* **New York: John Wiley and Sons, 1995.**
This is the story of a woman who had such a beautiful voice that she could have been an international star. Instead, she chose to live in her homeland. Her life took her from the South African countryside to England, Johannesburg, and Durban, where she worked as an interpreter and assistant to a doctor.

Parker, Linda J. *The San of Africa.* **Minneapolis: Lerner Publications Company, 2002.**
This is a profile of the San of southern Africa, describing their history, culture, religion, family life, language, economy, and their struggle to maintain their cultural traditions in the modern world.

Pascoe, Elaine. *South Africa: Troubled Land.* **Rev. ed. New York: Franklin Watts, 1992.**
This history book makes it easy to understand how apartheid came about and how it was overthrown.

Paton, Alan. *Cry, the Beloved Country.* **New York: Scribner, 1948.**
This beautifully written story of a black family and a white family brought together by tragedy is still the most widely read South African novel.

Shales, Melissa. *Fodor's Exploring South Africa.* **New York: Fodor's Travel Publications, 2000.**
This colorful travel guide takes the reader to the parks, museums, and off-the-beaten paths of South Africa and has lots of information on history, culture, and people.

Sunday Times.
Website: <http://www.suntimes.co.za> (May 6, 2003)
This website, updated daily, consists of the Johannesburg weekly newspaper. It carries in-depth reports on topics such as the impact of HIV/AIDS in South Africa, the history of the ANC, and how the "New South Africa" has affected peoples' lives.

vgsbooks.com.
Website: <http://www.vgsbooks.com>
Visit vgsbooks.com, the homepage of the Visual Geography Series®, which is updated regularly. You can get linked to all sorts of useful on-line information, including geographical, historical, demographic, cultural, and economic websites. The vgsbooks.com site is a great resource for late-breaking news and statistics.

Walker, Sally M. *Fossil Fish Found Alive!* **Minneapolis: Carolrhoda Books, Inc., 2002.**
This award-winning book tells the exciting story of the discovery of the coelacanth—a prehistoric fish that was thought to have been extinct for hundreds of thousands of years—off the coast of South Africa.

Captions for photos appearing on cover and chapter openers:

Cover: Signal Hill is a landmark in Cape Town.

pp. 4–5 The Wild Flower Garden in Ramskop Nature Reserve in Clanwilliam blazes with the colors of more than three hundred species of cultivated wildflowers.

pp. 8–9 A narrow dirt road allows vehicle traffic over a pass in the Drakensberg Range. Otherwise KwaZulu-Natal looks uninhabited from this high vantage point.

pp. 18–19 Early human inhabitants of South Africa expressed themselves in paintings on rock surfaces. One such find is estimated to be seventy-seven thousand years old, compared with the next oldest cave paintings, which were made some forty thousand years ago.

pp. 36–37 Students from Johannesburg await live demonstrations of Ndebele culture at the Open Air Museum at Botshabelo Historical Village in Middelburg, Mpumalanga.

pp. 46–47 A Christian Indian wedding party in Durban poses for a photographer.

pp. 58–59 Johannesburg glitters in the twilight.

Photo Acknowledgments

The photographs in this book are reproduced with the permission of: © Gerald Cubitt, pp. 4–5, 14 (bottom), 25 (top), 38, 45, 46–47, 51, 57, 61, 62; © Digital Cartographics, pp. 6, 13; © Reuters NewMedia Inc./CORBIS, pp. 7, 26; © Anita Brosius-Scott, pp. 8–9, 10, 11, 14 (top), 17, 36–37, 43, 56, 63, 65; South African Tourism Board, pp. 12, 58–59; © L. Reemer/TRIP, p. 15 © Shaen Adey; Gallo Images/CORBIS, pp. 18–19; Mary Marks, p. 20; © Van der Heyden, pp. 21, 23, 42-43, 53 (left), 54; © Mary Evans Picture Library, p. 22; © Bettmann/CORBIS, pp. 25 (bottom), 29, 31, 32; © Rykoff Collection/ CORBIS, p. 28; © Phil Porter, p. 30; © TRIP/TRIP, pp. 33, 34; © M. Barlow/TRIP, pp. 40, 64; © Ask Images/TRIP, p. 44; © BASSOULS SOPHIE/CORBIS SYGMA, p. 48; © Anthony Bannister; Gallo Images/COR-BIS, p. 49; © Todd Strand/Independent Picture Service, pp. 52, 68; © D. Burrows/TRIP, p. 53 (right); © R. Spurr/TRIP, p. 60.

Cover photo: © Gerald Cubitt. Back cover photo: NASA.